BRITAIN IN OLD PHOTOGRAPHS

Made in Belfast

Trevor Parkhill
& Vivienne Pollock

NATIONAL MUSEUMS NORTHERN IRELAND

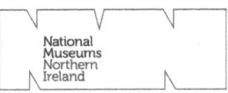

First published in 2005 by
Sutton Publishing

Reprinted in 2008 by
The History Press
The Mill, Brimscombe Port,
Stroud, Gloucestershire, GL5 2QG
www.thehistorypress.co.uk

Reprinted 2010, 2011, 2012, 2013

Copyright © National Museums Northern Ireland, 2010

All rights reserved. No part of this publication may be reproduced, stored in a retrieval system, or transmitted, in any form, or by any means, electronic, mechanical, photocopying, recording or otherwise, without the prior permission of the publisher and copyright holder.

British Library Cataloguing in Publication Data
A catalogue record for this book is available from the British Library.

ISBN 978-0-7509-4032-0

Typeset in 10.5/13.5 Photina.
Typesetting and origination by
Sutton Publishing Limited.
Printed and bound in England.

City street entertainment, in the shape of two women travellers and their hurdy-gurdy pictured in Belfast's Markets area in 1900. Horse-drawn carousels, Punch and Judy shows, performing dogs, bears and monkeys, ballad singers, jugglers, acrobats and fire-eaters were other popular street acts and entertainments. *(Y8583)*

Contents

	Introduction	5
1.	Shaping the City	9
2.	Four Giants	27
3.	Home Markets	51
4.	Street Level	73
5.	At Your Service	85
6.	For Entertainment and Delight	109
	Acknowledgements	128

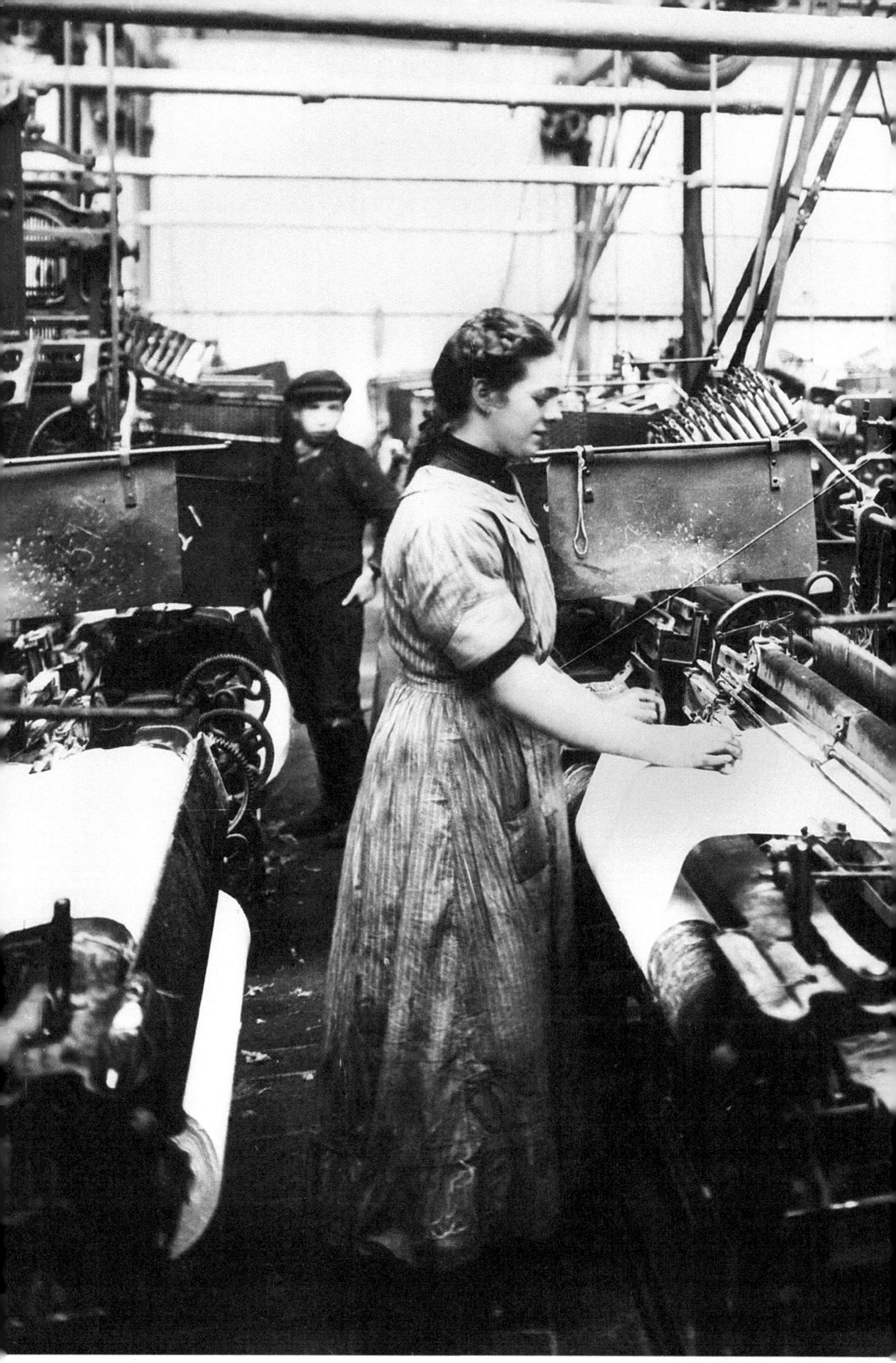

INTRODUCTION

The town and port of Belfast had a thriving merchant and trading community from the eighteenth century – in 1783 the first Chamber of Commerce in Ireland, and the second, after Leeds, in the British Isles, was founded here – but its importance as a centre for industry and manufacture dates essentially from the mid-nineteenth century. Its industrial might was based on the production of linen cloth and the construction of ships, enterprises which themselves provided the impetus for the emergence of a host of allied trades and functions, such as engineering, metal founding, chandlering and ropemaking. The rise of these industries encouraged people to move to Belfast – from elsewhere in Ireland and from further afield, a flow of population made more intense by the cataclysmic rural deprivation of the Famine period and the agricultural dislocation that followed. Belfast was home to 20,000 people in 1800; over the next century its population grew more steeply and more quickly than any other city in Britain and Ireland, standing at 70,000 in 1841, 121,000 in 1861 and 208,000 in 1881, before topping 350,000 souls by 1900.

This expansion of industry and population was matched by urban growth, as the town boundary, fixed in the 1830s to enclose 2½ square miles, was extended to encompass 23 square miles by the end of the century. By then, Belfast boasted the biggest port in Ireland in terms of the volume and value of trade, and the biggest linen factories, the largest ropeworks and the greatest tonnage production of ships in the world. In 1888 Belfast was officially accorded the status of City; its magnificent new City Hall, formally opened in 1906 on the site of the town's old White Linen Hall, embodied both its solidity and its pride.

Right: The City Hall photographed shortly after it opened. *(Y1985)*

Opposite: Girl operating power looms in the Brookfield Linen Company on the Crumlin Road, c. 1900. *(H10/31/15, detail)*

The photographs in this book focus on work as the beating heart of Belfast. We look first at the expansion of the city, with the construction of its great mills, shopping and trading emporiums and public buildings; the establishment of communications and transport links; and the introduction and improvement of public amenities. We then turn to the industrial giants and the firms that made them so mighty – the two shipyards, some of the two hundred linen manufacturers and thirty-four bleaching and dyeing businesses, the foundries and engineering firms and the ropeworks – before considering smaller, but, to the people who worked in them, no less important, concerns involved in the manufacture of commodities and consumables.

Belfast, with its abundance of freshwater springs of exceptional purity, was a world centre for aerated water production, and for brewing and distilling. Sixty per cent of all the whiskey produced in Ireland was exported through Belfast, with Dunville's, one of its major distillers, boasting of sending to the Treasury 'the largest cheque for duty on anything ever paid to the imperial revenue either through the Customs or the Excise' in respect of the £50,572 8s 2d they paid in 1895 as the duty on 688,056 bottles of Dunville's 'Special Liqueur' and 'V.R.' whiskey. Belfast-made mineral waters were sold across the globe; Cantrell & Cochrane, famous in later years for their 'big, big bottles', produced ginger ale, fruit-flavoured lemonades, club soda, seltzer and kali waters which were described as 'sparkling like champagne . . . but not leaving, as champagne does so often, repentance and self-reproach as a heritage of the morrow'. Indulgence in tobacco-taking was served by the world-famous brands of pipe tobacco, snuff and cigarettes produced at Murray's and Gallaher's and with the clay pipes that were made in their thousands at Hamilton's historic factory.

The busy junction of Castle Place, *c.* 1907. (*W10.21.14*)

A city needs to eat, and Belfast had a series of impressive bakeries, beginning with Bernard Hughes's mill – home of 'Barney's Baps', progenitors of the now-famous Belfast bap – where the imposing Hungarian rollers worked six days per week. Firms such as Inglis and Ormeau produced a variety of breads for city and country dwellers alike; fancier tastes were tickled with biscuits and cakes made by Marsh's and similar outlets. New food products were developed by concerns such as Newforge Foods, which specialised in meat, particularly pork processing, while Belfast Co-operatives were key suppliers of flour, bread and, significantly, clean milk. Tea and coffee were imported and sold in huge quantities by local merchants such as Forster Green, who paid as much attention to good works as to his business and whose name lives on in the hospital he endowed for the treatment of tuberculosis. In the city streets, restaurants and cafés competed for the custom of passers-by, while both commercial and family hotels offered home comforts to visitors.

It was at street level too that a growing diversity of shops and retail outlets – large and small – tempted the casual as well as the dedicated shopper, with local branches of national chains, such as Dewhurst's, Lipton's and Austin Reed's beginning to feature more prominently. Many of the city's own best-loved stores pictured in the following pages – Hogg's high-class china and glass suppliers, Robinson & Cleaver's linen warehouse and Arnott's opulent multi-floored department store to name three examples – have since closed, envisioned only in memory and recalled by precious heirlooms once purchased there to mark weddings, anniversaries and other important occasions.

As the city grew and the needs of its industries became more demanding, a range of agencies emerged to offer training and vocational support. Technical classes, industrial schools, apprenticeships and pre-apprenticeships all played a part in helping young men and women gain a foot on the ladder, while philanthropic and charitable societies provided a vital lifeline for those who had lost their hold or failed to find it. Medical and health services such as dentistry and eye care expanded and improved, while Belfast's Queen's University established itself as a key player in the fields of medical research and the development of medical technologies. Industrial associations sprang up to increase interest in and markets for home-produced goods; workers began to organise in trades unions, to the dismay of many employers.

In its final section this book looks at what would now be termed the creative and leisure industries. Belfast produced fine artists, such as William Conor and John Vinycombe, both of whom served their time working for local printers and publishers. Marcus Ward, where Vinycombe worked as a chief designer, were one of the commercial pioneers of the Christmas card as well as the inventor of the tear-off calendar. Theatres flourished, the cinema, radio and television arrived, Belfast Museum and Art Gallery got a stately new home and the magnificent Palm House in the Botanic Gardens was completed and centrally heated with stoves and piping produced in the city at Musgrave's Falls Foundry. The streets themselves buzzed with the activity of entertainers, street theatre, funfairs and kerbside traders.

With one exception – the depiction of the William Conor painting of Belfast women brushing their doorsteps, which is taken from the collections of our sister institution, the Ulster Folk and Transport Museum – all the images contained in this volume represent material held at the Ulster Museum and curated by the History Department. The greatest proportion of the photographs included reflect the work of A.R. Hogg, who operated in the city from the 1880s until his death in 1939 and who acted as official photographer for the Workman Clark & Co. shipyard as well as undertaking shorter-term commissions for numerous local businesses and shops, charitable concerns and philanthropic campaigns. The work of R.J. Welch, official photographer to Harland & Wolff, also features prominently. In addition, we have taken the opportunity to publish images taken from our extensive collections of trade catalogues, engraved letterheads and other printed promotional material.

As far as possible we have tried to focus on the people, the great majority of them un-named in the archives, whose energy, dedication and imagination fuelled the industrial, commercial and corporate expansion of Belfast in the years up to the outbreak of the Second World War. Photographs cannot, of course, convey the noise, the dust, the smell, the danger and the dirt, the physical grind and the sheer drudgery that characterised so much of the work shown in these pages. Life was hard for working people in Belfast during the years covered here, as it was for working people everywhere. The images portrayed in this book are testimony to their resilience, their skills, their tenacity and their resourcefulness.

A particularly fine printed letterhead produced by the Belfast firm of W&G Baird Ltd. *(G9DC5203)*

1

Shaping the City

Belfast received its first electricity supply from a small, makeshift station in Chapel Lane in 1895, which provided power only for street lights. Within three years demand had so far outstripped supply that work commenced to build a massive power station in East Bridge Street, where this photograph of an engineering squad and their emergency van was taken in November 1938. *(Y3073)*

Breaking ice on the Lagan Canal, Belfast, January 1895. It is a sign of the relatively late development of Belfast as a major industrial and commercial centre that, although the lower valley of the River Lagan provided a natural routeway from Lough Neagh to the head of Belfast Lough, it was not until 1793, some sixty years after work had begun on Ireland's first canal, that a navigable cut was built to link the city with its lowland hinterland. The canal closed quietly in 1958, when the Ministry of Commerce announced that its lower reaches, between the first locks at Stranmillis and the Union Locks at Sprucefield, near Lisburn, were to be abandoned, having been unused by boats for some time. *(Y5706)*

Barges moored at Belfast's Sand Quay, to the south of Queen's Bridge, 1890. Coal was the most important commodity carried from the port, with grain a close second. The main downstream traffic consisted of washed sand and gravel for building purposes in Belfast, followed by native timber, peat moss, fireclay goods, bricks and agricultural produce. Uniquely in Ireland, the boats that worked the Lagan and other Ulster waterways were known as lighters, and the families of the lightermen travelled with them. Although they carried sails, the lighters depended for draught on horses, whose drivers were paid £2 for hauling a boat from Belfast to Lough Neagh. This trip took two days if all went well; if the boat was light, the journey-time was reduced to 12 hours and drivers could expect to earn only 10s. *(W10/29/34)*

Potatoes being inspected by the Ministry of Agriculture at Clarendon Dock, January 1938, before exportation to England. *(Y2260)*

Clarendon Dock, September 1917, with the Bristol and London warehousing sheds in the background. Two sailing ships are moored alongside, one of which appears to be Norwegian. One of the many tugs that aided such ocean-going ships through the tortuous approaches to Belfast Harbour, together with its captain, or pilot, takes pride of place in the foreground. *(Y2294)*

Heysham Dock, 1938, showing men using one of Belfast Docks' huge, movable electric cranes to unload a container, presumably full of furniture, and household effects, from the hold of a passenger ship. The Lancashire port of Heysham provided one of the principal shipping and cargo connections between Belfast and Britain until the 1970s. *(Y2272)*

Opposite: Belfast Harbour Commissioners' barge and workmen laying electrical cable across Victoria Channel to West Twin Island, August 1938. *(H10/21/664)*

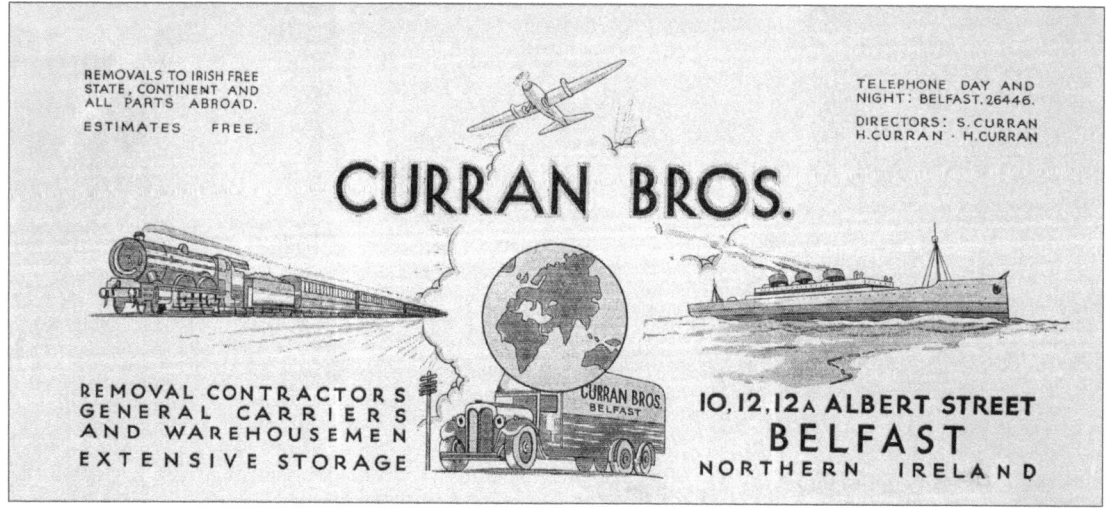

Advertisement for Curran Brothers, Removers and General Carriers, showing the many ways this firm was able to transport your belongings across the globe. *(GD9DC5193)*

Between the basalt ridge of Belfast's Cave Hill and the Triassic sandstone and marl that support it lies a broad layer of chalk and greensand, an important source of lime for agriculture and building purposes. This rare photograph of the interior of the Cavehill Lime Quarries by the Belfast photographer A.R. Hogg was taken as part of one of his many experiments with early flashlight photography. *(Y8574)*

This ancient oak structure, unearthed during excavations of McGladdry's brickworks on the Springfield Road in July 1930, is possibly the remains of part of the eighteenth-century man-made system which brought clean water to the centre of Belfast through a series of wooden pipes and conduits from sources to the south and west. *(W10/04/04)*

Printed plumber's billhead, designed by the Belfast firm of Marcus Ward and carrying a marvellously detailed engraving of a water closet. By this time, the population of the city had swelled to over 70,000 souls and demand for water for domestic purposes, let alone for industry and commerce, had grown to such an extent that the newly formed Water Commission were warned that by 1861 they would face an estimated daily deficit of almost a million gallons for households alone. *(G9DC5201)*

The team who built Belfast's new Woolworth's 'super store and cafeteria' on the corner of High Street and Cornmarket, pictured on the roof of the completed building in May 1930. *(Y2395)*

The building seven months previously, promising that at least part of the new premises will be open temporarily for Christmas trading. *(Y2390)*

Team of hodsmen working on the construction of the Donegall Road Linen Factory in 1902. *(Y8608)*

This busy scene, photographed in October 1931, shows the foundations of the new Automatic Telephone Exchange and Telephone House being laid at the corner of May Street and Cromac Street. *(Y3021)*

The premises of Thomas Dixon & Sons, also known as the Ulster Saw Mills & Creosoting Works, in Milewater Road, photographed in 1905. According to the Trades Directory, by 1909 Thomas Dixon also traded from extensive premises at Corporation Street, while maintaining the works shown above and others at King Street, Great George's Street and York Street. The firm was one of almost forty sawmills and timber merchants operating in Belfast at this time, such was the city's demand for wood for building and manufacturing purposes. *(Y2469, detail)*

Although better known as a builder and building supplier, the Belfast firm of J.P. Corry, whose promotional campaign in 1937 included a display of the eight different types of slate available from them with each one mounted on its own miniature model roof, were also major timber specialists with a surprisingly diverse product list, as the advertisements pictured opposite reveal. *(Y1853)*

Corry's advertisement for pulpits, on which many a bible was thumped! *(G9DC5169)*

Corry's advertisement for reading desks. *(G9DC5167)*

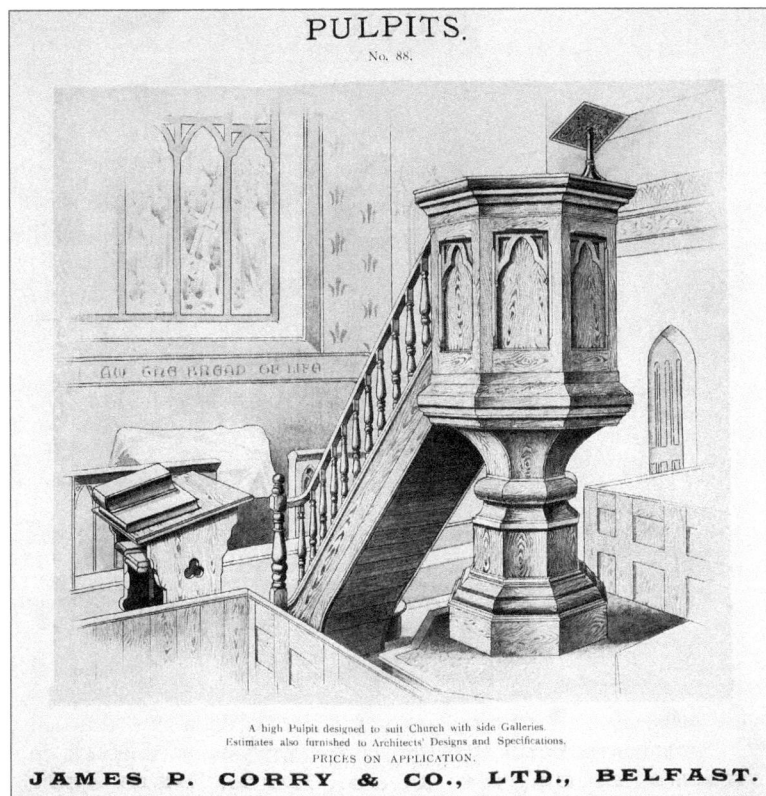

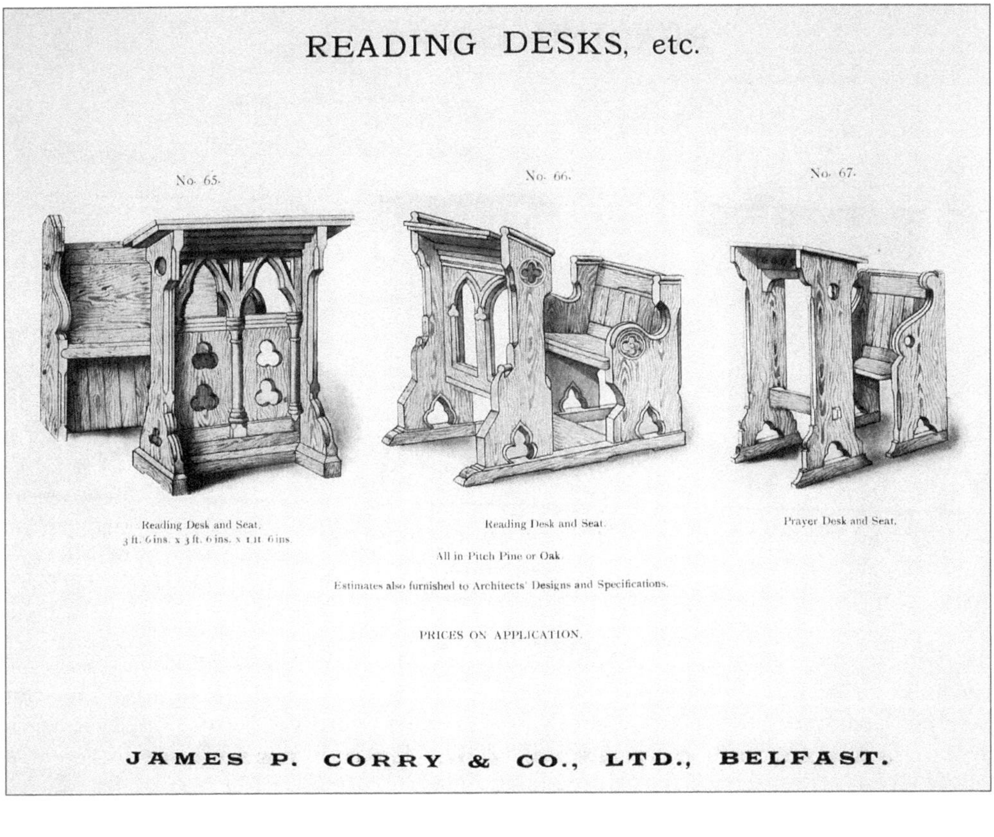

Men laying cobbles outside the Ulster Unionist Offices in Belfast's Arthur Square, August 1911. This was an arduous task, but essential for the free flow of horse-drawn traffic, which was much less likely to skid on such a textured surface. *(Y391634)*

Taken in June 1926, this photograph shows men breaking up foundations to erect the statue of Sir Edward Harland, seen in the background to the right, in the grounds of Belfast's City Hall. The statue was made by Thomas Brock, who also sculpted the statue of Queen Victoria which stands nearby. The dilapidated building behind them is the old Linen Hall Hotel. *(Y391632)*

Mr James Miller, saddler, resplendent in apron, photographed at the door of his shop at 142 Cromac Street in February 1912. A set of cart harness is displayed outside, while the door to his dwelling house carries a depiction of a prancing charger. *(W10/29/6)*

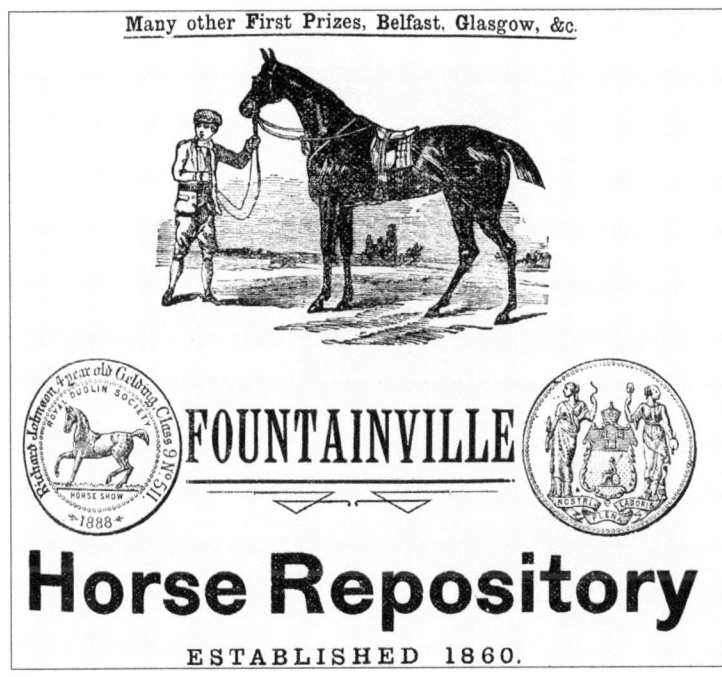

The logo from Richard Johnson's advertisement for his horse-dealing business, which promised to have 'always a stock of High-Class Horses, Hunters, Match Carriage Horses, Polo Ponies . . . All selected with care and judgement in the best Southern Fairs' and subject to veterinary opinion, presumably that of his brother, William Johnson, who conveniently occupied the premises next door. *(Fountainville)*

Although Belfast's Water Commissioners had agreed in 1858 to the request of the newly formed Royal Society for the Prevention of Cruelty to Animals to supply troughs of water free of charge for Belfast's workhorses, supplies of piped water to the city were so unreliable that carts carrying fresh clean drinking water for all the city's thirsty inhabitants were a familiar sight until well into the twentieth century. Here a fine pair of matched greys draws along tramlines one of the big watering carts used by the tramway to water the hundreds of horses that worked hard pulling Belfast's trams until the system was electrified in 1907. *(Y8528)*

In one end, out the other? In a city of horses, this sweeper, or scavenger as they were known, provided an essential function in keeping the roadways clear. The fruits of his labour were not without value, feeding city allotments and gardens. In the background can be seen one of the city's open-top horse trams, waiting for business in Donegall Place. *(Y8564)*

Victoria Street, during reconstruction of the tramway, March 1925. This view of men at work is taken from an advertising postcard extolling the virtues of 'Lightning Brand' Aluminous Cement which allowed the supplying contractors, Norman Macnaughton & Sons of Belfast, to start paving only 12 hours after the concrete had been laid in place. *(Y6802)*

Belfast Corporation Tramways conductor, on the left with his ticket machine and money bag, and the especially cheery driver Mr Grady. *(Y8289)*

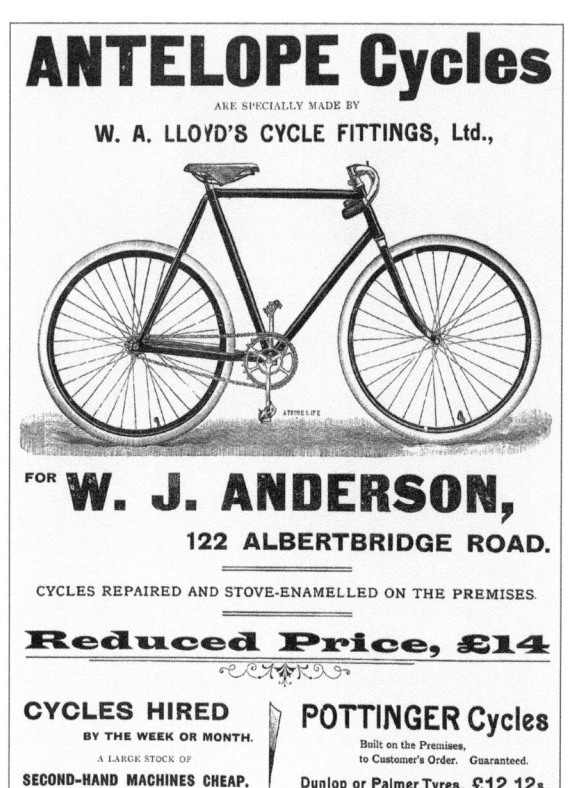

Left: Advertisement for Anderson's bicycle shop on Belfast's Albertbridge Road, from the 1906 Belfast Street Directory. *(AD6)*

Opposite: The world-famous inventor of the pneumatic tyre, John Boyd Dunlop was a veterinary surgeon who set up practice in May Street, Belfast, in the 1860s. According to the story, he thought of his idea for an inflated rubber tyre in 1887, while watching his young son riding his tricycle over the cobbled streets outside his house. After some experimentation he fashioned tyres from tubes of sheet rubber covered with linen, which he blew up with a football pump and tied to the wheels. He patented his idea and went into partnership with the Belfast cycle makers W. Edlin, who had a factory in Smithfield, before setting up on his own in 1890 with the Dunlop Tyre and Rubber Company. *(Dunlop)*

Bicycles were not only used for recreational and personal purposes; they were also an important means of transport and carriage in the commercial and service sectors. Here, a well turned out message boy in gaiters and gleaming boots stops on Lombard Street to chat to two mates, the younger of whom is holding several tin cans of a type customarily used to carry tea for workers' refreshment. Behind them is parked an early motor car. *(Y2446, detail)*

Mr Pyper, manager of Wood Milne's tyre depot in Donegall Square West, sits proudly in his firm's magnificent Napier car in Victoria Square in March 1918. Note the advertising the car carries on its bonnet and spare tyre. *(Y2692)*

As this advertisement from 1909 indicates, hiring a car at this time meant hiring a smartly uniformed driver as well! One wonders, perhaps, what the 'every modern convenience' Ferguson's cars came equipped with actually represented. *(Ferguson Ltd)*

2

Four Giants

A group of workers from Spence, Bryson & Co.'s Loopbridge Weaving Factory on Lismore Street, off the Ormeau Road, pose for their photograph under decorations put up for the coronation of King George VI. This is one of a series of images of workers at this factory produced by A.R. Hogg on 12 May 1937. *(H10/60/7)*

Another Hogg photograph of linen workers, this time the office staff and departmental heads at the Clonard Mill premises of William Ross and Co., Flax and Tow Spinners. *(H10/36/5)*

Staff of the weaving department of Thompson Rogers & Co.'s linen factory in what appears to be a relatively early photograph of industrial workers. The name of the firm has been spelled out in white card resting on the punch cards which conveyed the pattern to damask looms. The staff are surrounded by rolls of cloth and the women seated in the front row all carry loaded shuttles. *(Y8111)*

The imposing form of Jennymount Mill on North Derby Street, photographed here in 1908, looms over the little girl gazing up at it in the foreground, perhaps imagining the day when she will, in all probability, start to work there. *(H10/35/25)*

Hemp reeling, William Ewart & Son's Mountain Mill on the Legoniel Road, October 1930. *(H10/50/25)*

The dressing shop at William Ewart & Son's Crumlin Road Mill, Crumlin Road, October 1930. *(H10/31/20)*

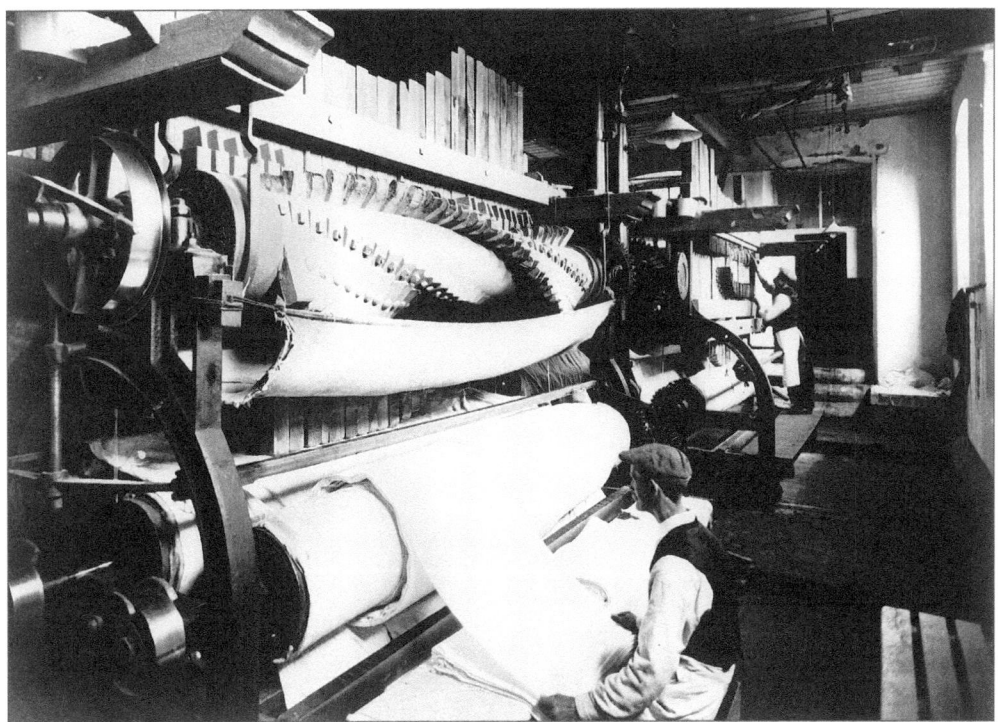
Beetling linen cloth, William Ewart & Son's Glenbank Bleachworks, October 1930. *(H10/50/13)*

White lapping room, York Street Flax Spinning Company, York Street. Linen cloth was lapped, that is, folded in pleats along its length, so that it could be opened like a book to allow more easily every inch to be examined for quality. The lapped cloth can be seen in piles on the table in the foreground. *(W10/21/291)*

Measuring and rolling machines, York Street Flax Spinning Company, Belfast. Although the workforce of factory-based linen production was predominantly female, there were some male bastions, such as mechanics, supervising and quality control, as indicated in this photograph, where the man standing in the centre appears to be examining the cloth minutely as it passes through the rollers he tends. *(W10/21/290)*

Apart from bleaching the cloth, at its bleach-works in Muckamore, Co. Antrim, every aspect of linen production from raw flax to finished cloth was achieved within the huge premises of the York Street Mill, where there were also departments to add value to the end product. This image shows the handkerchief-ornamenting room, with its quiet rows of busy-fingered, well turned out young girls. *(W10/21/294)*

Ross Brothers' factory, Bloomfield Avenue, June 1927, showing a girl working at a power-driven damask loom and the huge loops of punch cards which carried the design to the weave. The women who tended these machines would each have been responsible for two or three of these monsters. *(H10/06/06)*

The spinning room of the Ulster Spinning Company Ltd, at Linfield Mill on the Linfield Road. *(10/29/168)*

The photograph (left) gives some impression of the crowded conditions and vast spaces that spinners worked in, but shows little of the unpleasantness of factory flax-spinning. The nature of the process made the spinning room extremely hot and humid, and the machine operators were drenched with water as the soaked fibre was twisted around the spindles. Workers were especially prone to bronchitis and other pulmonary illnesses, while the hot and noisy conditions also gave rise to a disorder known as mill fever, which produced severe headaches and nausea and persisted until workers became acclimatised to their surroundings.

Mill workers worked long hours for low pay, particularly in the case of the thousands of women who made up the bulk of the labour force. In 1906, for example, their average pay stood at 10s 9d per week, compared with 22s 4d paid to men. On top of that was a punitive system of fines and deductions for poor work and disciplinary offences, which led one of the first women factory inspectors to remark that some young women could work all week for as little as 5 or 6 shillings.

As shown by their message to 'the linen slaves of Belfast', the Irish Trades Union movement did mobilise in support of mill workers. Gradually, as the twentieth century progressed, both pay and conditions improved. *(DSC1678)*

Irish Textile Workers' Union

(Textile Section: Irish Women Workers' Union).

Headquarters—Liberty Hall, Dublin.

TO THE
LINEN SLAVES OF BELFAST.

FELLOW-WORKERS,

OUR condition, and the condition of the sweated women of all classes of labour in Belfast, has recently become the subject of discussion on all the political platforms of England, and of long articles in all the most widely read newspapers and magazines of both countries. Almost unanimously they agree in condemning the conditions under which you work, your miserable wages, the abominable system of fining which prevails, and the slaughtering speed at which you are driven. It is pointed out that the conditions of your toil are unnecessarily hard, that your low wages do not enable you to procure sufficiently nourishing food for yourselves or your children, and that as a result of your hard work, combined with low wages, you are the easy victims of disease, and that your children never get a decent chance in life, but are handicapped in the race of life before they are born.

All this is to-day admitted by every right-thinking man and woman in these Islands. **Many Belfast Mills are slaughter-houses for the women and penitentiaries for the children.** But while all the world is deploring your conditions, they also unite in deploring your slavish and servile nature in submitting to them; they unite in wondering of what material these Belfast women are made, who refuse to unite together and fight to better their conditions.

Irish men have proven themselves to be heroes in fighting to abolish the tyranny of landlordism. Irish women fought heroically in the same cause. Are the Irish working women of Belfast not of the same race? Can they not unite to fight the slavery of capitalism as courageously as their sisters on the farms of Ireland united to fight the slavery of Irish landlordism? **Public opinion**

The big Belfast store of Robinson & Cleaver's was famous worldwide for the supply of fine linens, but also produced its own quality fabrics. Here, in an echo of times before factories and mills, a male handloom weaver sits at work in one of its shops. *(W10/21/55)*

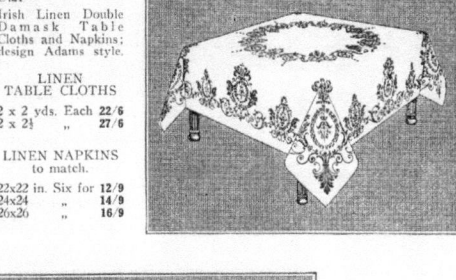

A notice for one of Robinson & Cleaver's autumn sales, complete with a testimonial from the West Indies. *(G9DC5204)*

Another highly skilled task in the linen industry was the hand-painting of damask cloth, as these women are doing. *(Y5730)*

W. Smyth & Son's Irish Linen House in College Street, photographed in 1934. In the centre of the window can be seen what appears to be a painted damask tablecloth, selling for the princely sum of 10*s* 6*d*. *(Y1831)*

Belfast's College of Technology was a key provider of training in the mechanical and material skills required by the local linen industry. It also provided an important platform for the celebration of those skills and the industry they supported, as this image of its float 'Miss Belfast 1927' in a linen industry parade demonstrates. *(HP10/21a)*

Even the most basic advertising of some of the big Belfast linen concerns constituted minor works of art – this notice listing some of the most pre-eminent clients of the Belfast Damask and Linen Co. appeared in 1901, beautifully engraved with traditional damask patterns and motifs. *(DSC1676)*

Launch of the *City of Sydney* at Workman Clarke & Co.'s north yard, 2 October 1929, taken by A.R. Hogg, who was official photographer to ths historic firm between its revival in 1928 and when it went out of business in 1935. It launched its last ship in 1934. *(H10/21/638)*

South yard, Harland and Wolff shipyard, by their official photographer, R.J. Welch. This view shows the Hamilton graving dock and Harbour Pumping Station in the middle distance, and beyond that the long frontage of boiler shops and engine shops. *(W10/46/45)*

One of the drawing offices at Harland & Wolff, where the ships' plans were drawn up by teams of draughtsmen. The impressive building that housed these offices survives today as a listed structure. *(Y39044.5)*

One of the wood-polishing shops where ship fittings and furnishings, all constructed on site, were finished to required standards. Polishing was one of many carpentry trades and functions carried out at Harland & Wolff, including the storing and seasoning of huge wooden timbers and the erection of stocks and scaffolding; making pattern templates; and basic joinery, such as hanging doors and fitting stairs. *(Y39044.11)*

The huge draughting loft, where plans were drawn out in full scale before being made up into life-size wooden templates. Note the 'Belfast' roof, designed to maximise undisrupted floor space. *(Y39044.17)*

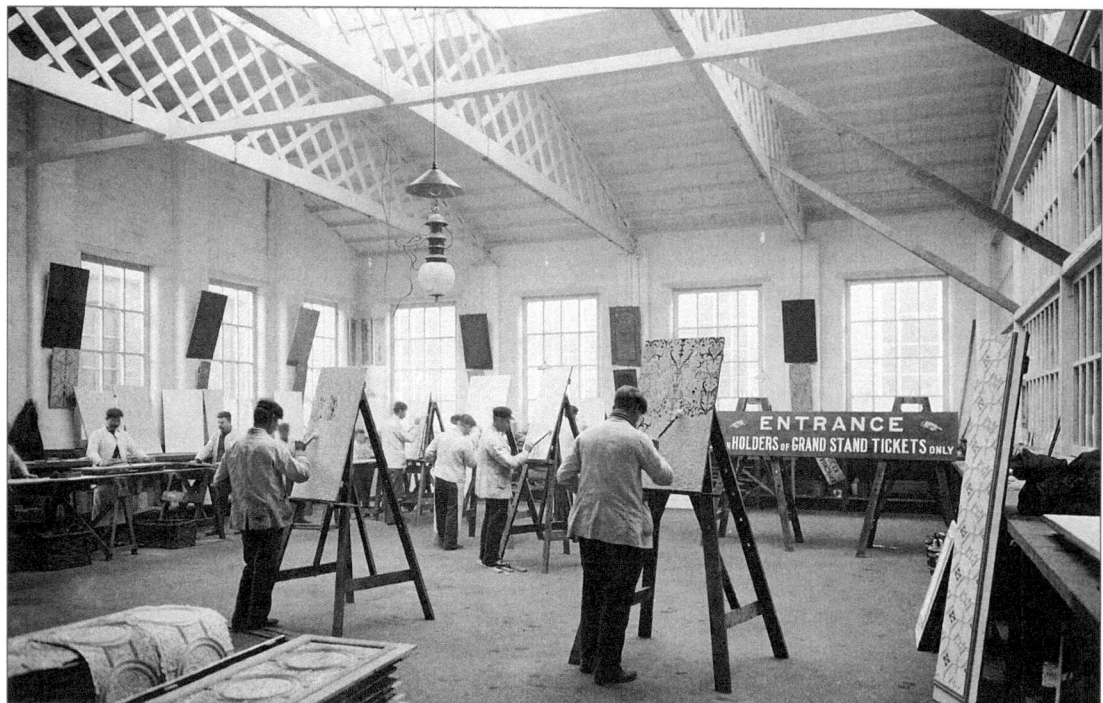

Harland and Wolff's artists' studio in 1899, with men hard at work painting wall panels for the interior of a White Star liner. The notice to the rear was for the launch ceremony of the *Teutonic* on 19 January 1889. *(Y39044.54)*

The engine pattern shop, 1899. Here the various parts of the engine were made in wood to be used to cast the final metal sections. *(Y39044.88)*

The interior of one of several huge bicycle sheds used by shipyard workers. *(Y39044.120)*

The platers' shop, with its magnificent Belfast roof, *c.* 1900. The moustachioed gentleman with the hammer in dead centre is David Mayne, who was apprenticed to the yard in 1888 at the age of fourteen and married seven years later when his training finished. Tragically, he died from diabetes three years after this photograph was taken. *(Y7295)*

This stunning image was taken from the floor of Thompson Graving Dock, and shows work being done on a massive propeller. *(W10/46/43)*

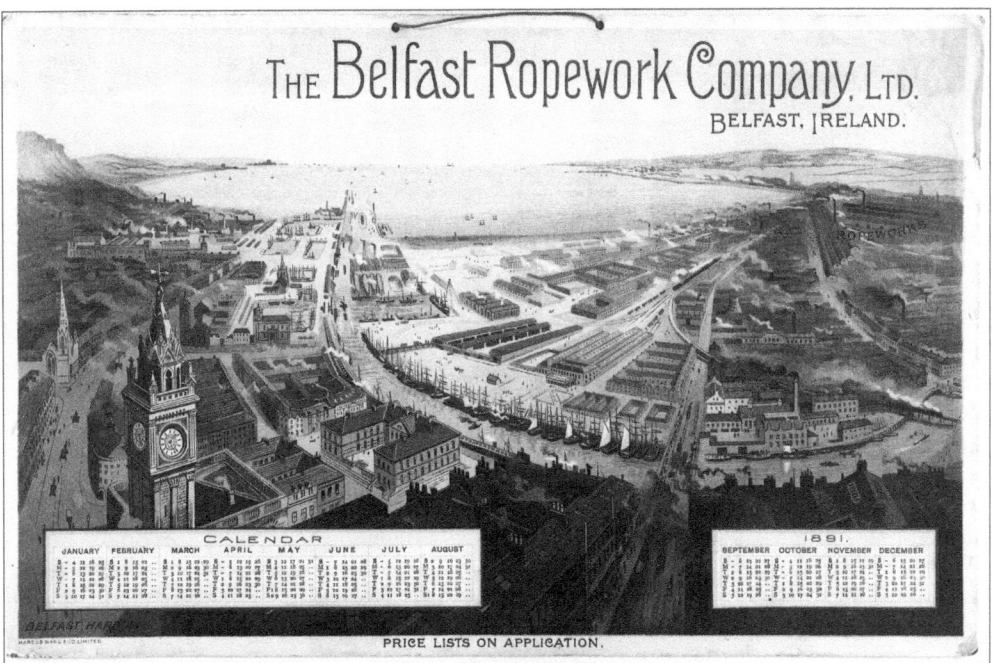

Image from the 1891 Belfast Ropeworks calendar showing Belfast Harbour and Docks, the sprawl of the shipyards and, in top centre right, the huge long sheds of Belfast Ropeworks, the biggest such manufacturer in the world at that time and one that sprang directly from Belfast's success as a centre for shipbuilding. *(Belfast Ropeworks)*

Flax rollers, Belfast Ropeworks, *c.* 1900. The Belfast Ropework Company was set up in 1872 by W. B. Lowson, partner in a firm of commission merchants and insurance agents; John Davison, a hemp and wire rope manufacturer, sailmaker and ships' chandler; Samuel Wilson, a flax spinner and merchant; and W. H. Smiles, the eldest son of the famous Victorian reformer and social theorist Samuel Smiles. A year later Gustav Wolff, of Harland & Wolff, bought into the firm and soon became its Chairman. *(Ropeworks)*

Some of the range of products made at Belfast Ropeworks, which included 'every description of rope and twine, from the largest cable to the finest fishing twine'. These were marketed across the world in such quantities that it was stated there was probably no port nor sailor in the world that was not familiar with them. *(Y391633)*

The Ropeworks also produced nets, which were mainly knitted by hand, as in this photograph of women making trawl nets for fishing. These complicated, bag-like structures were pieced together from a range of differently shaped pieces of net which incorporated a range of mesh sizes, and were impossible to make in entirety by machine. During the Second World War the women net-makers were kept busy producing camouflage nets. *(10/08/2)*

Mechanics department, Thos. Ferguson & Co. Ltd, Edenderry Factory, 1939. Although there was an Edenderry-based firm of bleachers called Ferguson in the nineteenth century, that concern closed in 1875. The famous textile firm of Thos. Ferguson & Co., to which this photograph may refer, was based in Banbridge and there is no record – save for this image – of it ever operating so close to Belfast. Perhaps the date holds the clue, and this Edenderry branch represented the short-lived dispersal of effort common to many companies in their drive to meet increased wartime demand for their products. *(Y8105)*

The factory-based linen industry, with its demand for machines and the skills to operate and maintain them, was, along with shipbuilding, a key player in the development of the engineering sector in Belfast. Other local enterprises played a similar role. Here, we see the tea room of the city's famous Sirocco Works, established in 1881 to make tea-drying machinery by Thomas Davidson as an offshoot of their tea plantation business. This was a pioneering venture, and Davidson's Sirocco Works soon grew into the largest manufacturer of machinery for tea estates in the world, as well as a world leader in the design and manufacture of machinery for ventilation and air conditioning and filtration. *(Y5845)*

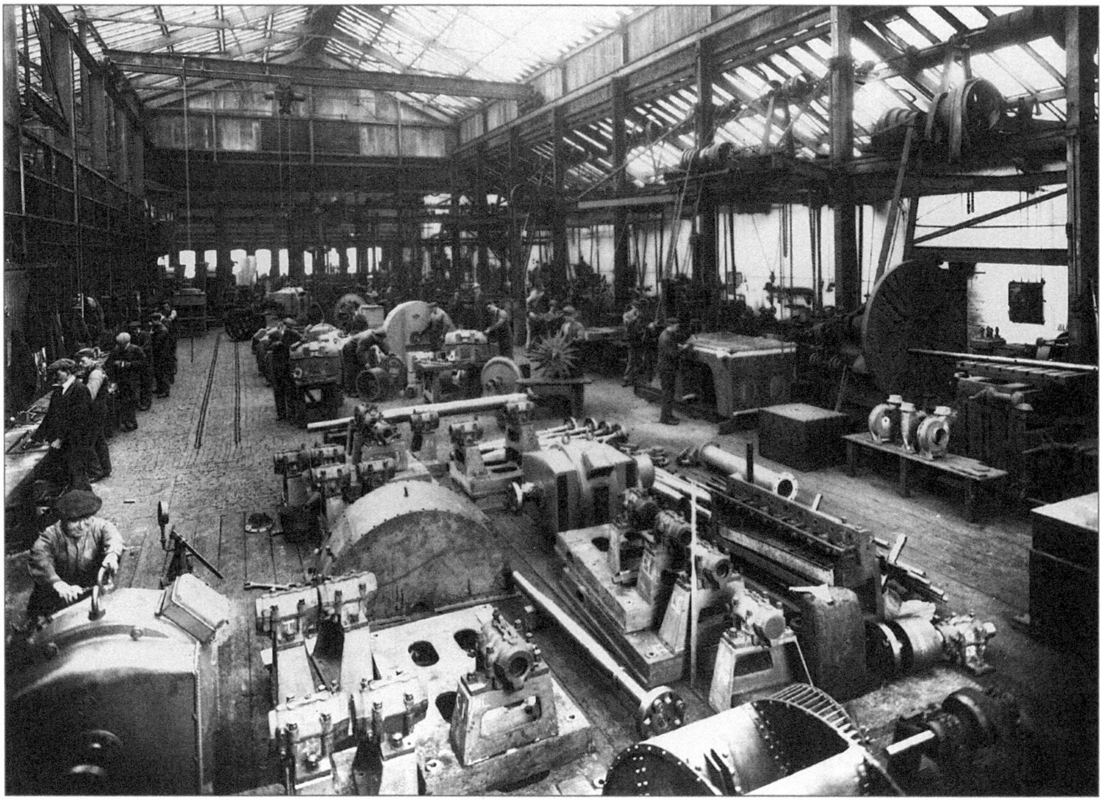

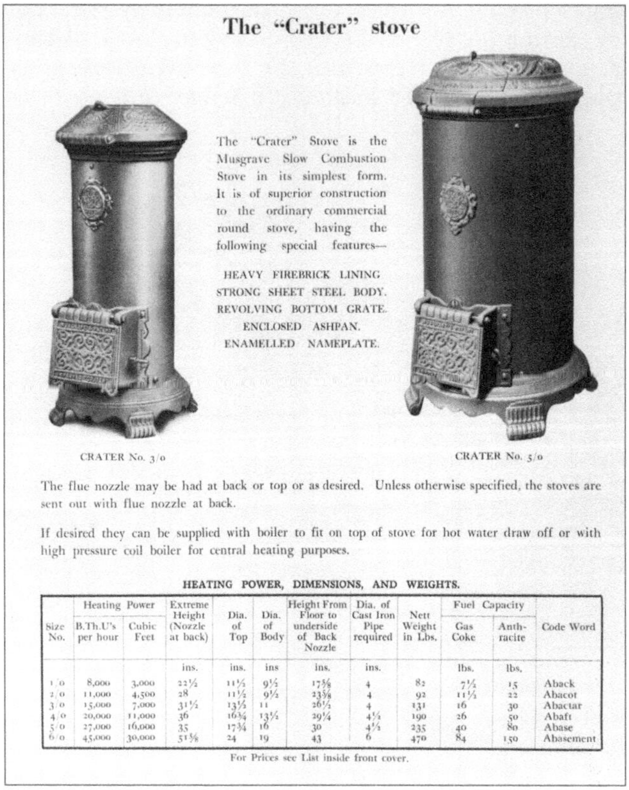

The "Crater" stove

The "Crater" Stove is the Musgrave Slow Combustion Stove in its simplest form. It is of superior construction to the ordinary commercial round stove, having the following special features—

HEAVY FIREBRICK LINING
STRONG SHEET STEEL BODY.
REVOLVING BOTTOM GRATE.
ENCLOSED ASHPAN.
ENAMELLED NAMEPLATE.

CRATER No. 3/0

CRATER No. 5/0

The flue nozzle may be had at back or top or as desired. Unless otherwise specified, the stoves are sent out with flue nozzle at back.

If desired they can be supplied with boiler to fit on top of stove for hot water draw off or with high pressure coil boiler for central heating purposes.

HEATING POWER, DIMENSIONS, AND WEIGHTS.

Size No.	Heating Power: B.Th.U's per hour	Heating Power: Cubic Feet	Extreme Height (Nozzle at back)	Dia. of Top	Dia. of Body	Height From Floor to underside of Back Nozzle	Dia. of Cast Iron Pipe required	Nett Weight in Lbs.	Fuel Capacity: Gas Coke	Fuel Capacity: Anth-racite	Code Word
			ins.	ins.	ins	ins.	ins.		lbs.	lbs.	
1/0	8,000	3,000	22½	11½	9½	17⅝	4	82	7½	15	Aback
2/0	11,000	4,500	28	11½	9½	23⅝	4	92	11½	22	Abacot
3/0	15,000	7,000	31½	13½	11	26½	4	131	16	30	Abactar
4/0	20,000	11,000	36	16¾	13½	29¼	4½	190	26	50	Abaft
5/0	27,000	16,000	35	17¾	16	30	4½	235	40	80	Abase
6/0	45,000	30,000	51⅝	24	19	43	6	470	84	150	Abasement

For Prices see List inside front cover.

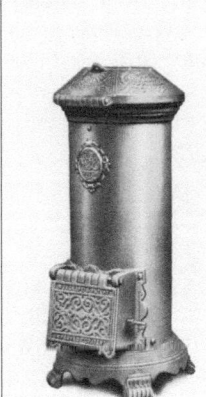

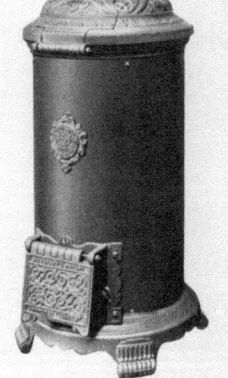

Above: The interior of one of the workshops of Musgrave & Sons, Iron Founders, on Belfast's Albertbridge Road, April 1931. This firm was established in 1855 and developed a strong catalogue of products, including an extremely popular and fashionable range of upmarket stable fittings and furniture. It was perhaps best known for its wonderful range of stoves, such as the 'Crater' advertised on the left, which sold like hot cakes (!) across Europe and beyond. *(Above: Y1573; Below: AD3)*

Opposite: Brass founding at the Combe Barbour's Falls Foundry in North Howard Street, August 1928. The Falls Foundry was established by James Combe in 1845 and specialised in the manufacture of machinery for the textile industry. It was also famous as being the world's first maker of grooved pulleys for rope-driving, a process invented by its founder, and as one of the first industrial premises in Ireland to be lit by electricity. *(Y3930)*

The huge Albert Foundry operated by the Belfast engineering firm of Mackies on the Springfield Road was also world-famous for the manufacture of textile machinery. Here, men operate one of their jute-softening machines. *(Mackies5)*

Like many of Belfast's big industries, Mackies assumed a key role in the manufacture of military supplies during the First World War. Here, some of its munitions workers display the fruits of their labour during that time. *(47/02/52)*

Opposite: The stop motion from a Mackies-made machine showing the level of high precision machine tooling achieved by the firm. Superimposed are four of the company's tool checks. These were handed in when workers collected their tools at the start of the day, and used at the end to tally tools returned against tools issued. *(Mackies1)*

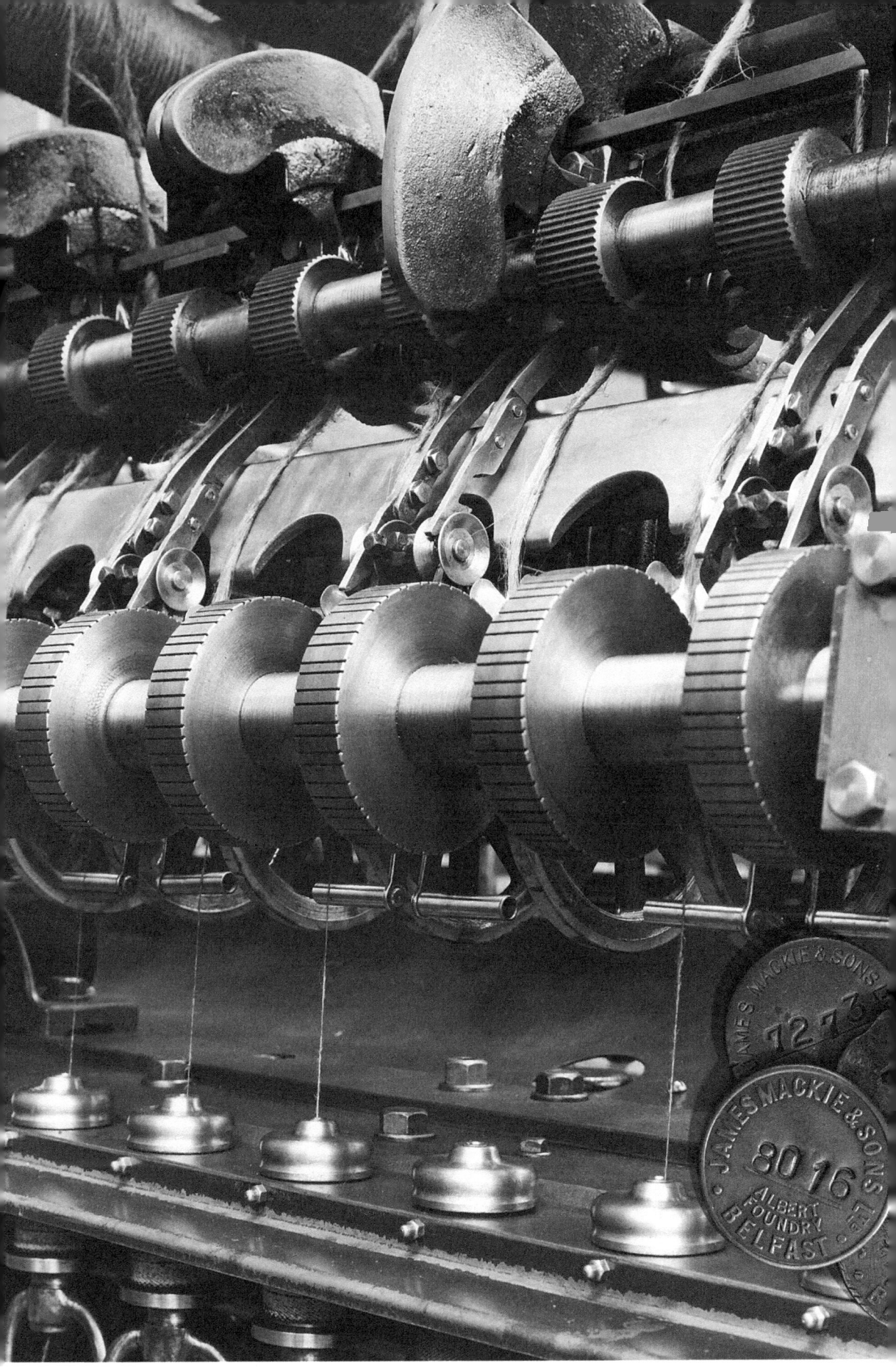

Advertisement for ironworker James Gray's agricultural machinery and prize-winning ploughs, which included his improved and much celebrated chilled plough and his world-famous lea and general plough, the latter of which brought him the patronage of Ireland's Lord Lieutenant and other noble gentlemen and farmers. *(AD7)*

3

Home Markets

Mr Magee, a farmer from Whiterock, just outside Belfast, with his horse and box sleigh loaded with manure for his fields, at the foot of a steep incline. Historically, Belfast was a working and trading city with strong rural roots, a population with close links to the soil, and immediately surrounded by productive farmland. Here, as in the rest of Northern Ireland, archaic farm conveyances, such as this sleigh, continued until within living memory to be used in hilly situations which more modern wheeled horse-drawn vehicles had great difficulty negotiating. *(Y10025)*

Premises of Cantrell & Cochrane, aerated water manufacturers, in Victoria Square, 1891. Victoria Square was the location of the celebrated Cromac Springs, which fed Belfast's world-famous mineral water industry. This factory had its own artesian well, sunk at a cost of £2,000, to ensure a permanent and abundant supply for its enterprise, which employed over 500 hands and exported thousands of bottles of sparkling beverages to thirsty customers around the world. *(Y391628)*

Founded in 1825, Grattan & Co. was the oldest concern in Belfast making aerated and mineral waters when this photograph of its premises in Great Victoria Street was taken in 1938. It was also the oldest extant apothecary's business in the city. The therapeutic benefits of Belfast's treated waters were much espoused in an era when the quality of many fresh water supplies – both at home and abroad – was doubtful, with Grattan's products reportedly winning favour with many eminent medical practitioners. *(Y3108)*

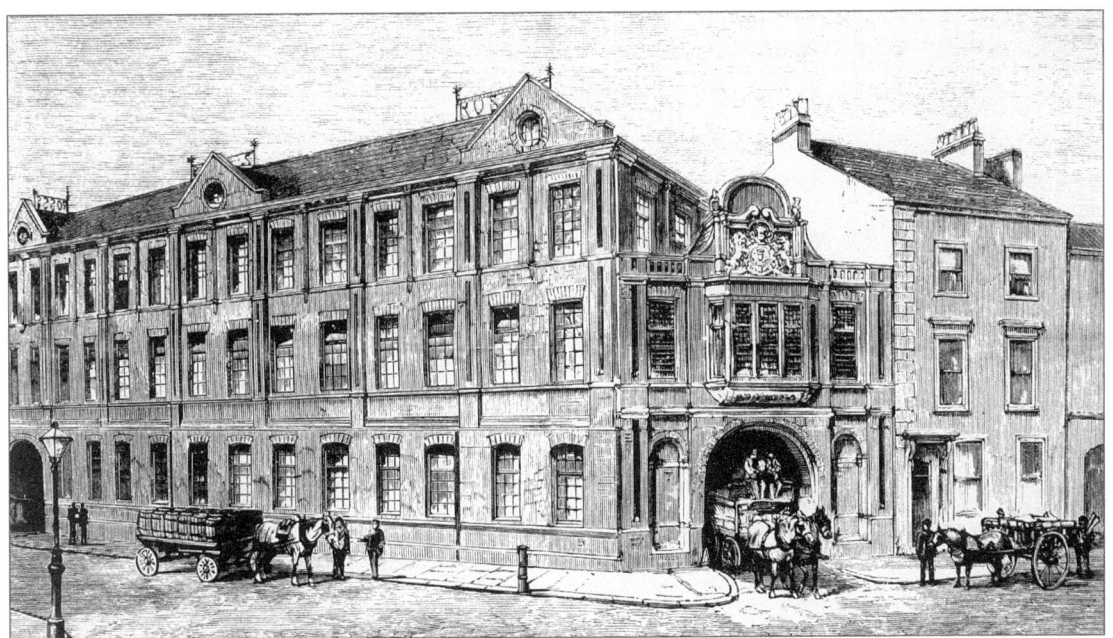

Established in 1879 by W.A. Ross, assisted by his son, the Royal Belfast Ginger Ale and Aerated Water Works (much better known just as 'Ross's') became world-famous for its Royal Ginger Ale: the ale's keeping qualities made it especially suitable for exportation and it quickly became as well known abroad as it was at home. It was particularly popular in tropical areas where cholera was endemic and fresh water deemed too hazardous to drink. *(10/21/317)*

The medicinal value of one of the products of this aerated water manufacturer on Belfast's Lisburn Road is clearly spelt out in its trade name which denotes a quinine-based tonic water effective against malaria. Again, Cromac Springs is hailed as the source of Wheeler's raw material, which was also used to make soda waters and ginger ale for consumption at home and abroad. *(Y3670)*

Workers posing on the occasion of the opening of Caffrey's new Mountain Brewery in Andersonstown in 1901. Caffrey's was famous for its stout, which was sold in spring-top rather than corked or capped bottles. Belfast was a major centre for brewing, which utilised the same springs of pure water exploited so profitably by the aerated water manufacturers. *(10/01/2)*

Women working as bottlers and labellers in J. & J. McConnell's breweries on Corporation Street in 1910. Again, the name 'Cromac' is displayed prominently on the advertising board behind the girl filling and capping bottles on the machine in the centre. McConnell's, whose directors when this photograph was taken included Charles Brett and Thomas Andrews, designer of the *Titanic*, also ran a distillery on Belfast's Ravenhill Road, with a bonded warehouse on Duncrue Street. *(HP10/21b)*

Mitchell & Co.'s Custom Bonded Stores on Great George's Street, with two horse-drawn drays and their drivers. This was one of several large bonded warehouses in Belfast, where precious stocks of whiskey aged and matured under the watchful guard of a resident excise officer. (W10/21/160)

The shop window of Forrester & Sons, wine and spirit merchants in Arthur Street, with its banners advertising the wares of Lyle & Kinahan Ltd (whose bonded stores were close by in Upper Arthur Street), photographed in 1937. One of the major players in the Belfast drinks industry, Lyle & Kinahan's were famous for their Kinahan's 'V.O.' Irish blended whiskey, for bottling ales and porters – they held a range of brands amounting to 80,000 gallons at any one time – and for dealing in wine and producing a variety of aerated waters. (Y1696)

The grounds of United Distillers on the Avoniel Road, after the demolition of the site in 1937. United Distillers took over the site of the old Connswater Spinning Co. in 1882 to exploit the artesian springs found there. Its collapse in 1937 was part of the enormous contraction of the Irish distilling industry engendered by the introduction of prohibition in America, its major export destination. This blow also caused the demise of Dunville's, one of the giants of Irish whiskey production, in the same year. (Y1579)

Hamilton's clay pipe factory, Bathurst Court, Durham Street, c. 1914. The man in this photograph is roughly shaping clay into pipe shapes before it is moulded. This factory, the longest lived of several in Belfast, was founded by Tom Hamilton in 1812 and produced thousands of these pipes each year as a cheap but decidedly fragile means of smoking. Ultimately disposable, the pipes were sold along with the tobacco they held in inns and public houses as well as tobacconists. Unlike their more expensive and elaborate wooden counterparts, they were used as enthusiastically by old women as by men, or so the many photographs of Irish grannies puffing on clay pipes would suggest. *(Y7045)*

Women trimming the shanks of clay pipes after moulding and before firing. Hamilton's went out of business in 1931, partly because the partition of Ireland closed markets in the south of Ireland which formed the greater part of their business, although pipes were exported as far away as America. An important trade was with the Army whose regiments commissioned batches of their own uniquely shaped and numbered pipes; pipes were also produced to advertise tobacco brands and political campaigns and allegiances. *(Y7047)*

The sprawling premises of Gallaher's, which occupied a whole block on Belfast's York Street and was probably the biggest tobacco and cigarette factory in the world. The factory was started by Tom Gallaher, a Derry man, who moved to Belfast in 1863 to expand the pipe tobacco business he had started in his native city at the age of seventeen. An insightful and forward-thinking businessman, he instigated annual buying tours of tobacco plantations in America to ensure a consistently high quality of supply, before establishing his own American properties to grow leaf for himself. He originally specialised in roll pipe tobacco, but quickly realised the opportunity that the female market for cigarettes afforded after the Duchess de Clermont-Tonnere stunned her friends at the Savoy Hotel in London in 1896 by becoming the first woman of distinction to light up in public. Gallaher's had premises in London's Holborn district and Clerkenwell Road and went on to manufacture some 150 different brands of roll, flake and plug pipe tobacco and some of the most well-known cigarette brands in the world, including Benson & Hedges, Silk Cut, Park Drive, Sobranie, Kensitas, du Maurier and Senior Service, in addition to the famous Gallaher's Greens, Reds and Blues. *(Y2839)*

Opposite, above: Weighing tobacco in Gallaher's bonded warehouse on Severn Street, 1937. In 1889, with output expanded enormously by the establishment of its huge York Street works, Gallaher's paid the British Exchequer over £450,000 in duty on imports to its Belfast warehouses alone. By 1900 it was estimated that the duty bill was running at over £12,000 per week, or a massive £750,000 for the year. *(Y3614)*

Opposite, below: Gallaher's, York Street, May 1937. The environment that these women tobacco strippers worked in was considerably brightened by the flags and bunting that bedecked every quarter of the York Street factory in celebration of the coronation of George VI. By the 1950s Gallaher's employed 2,000 people in Belfast alone, and many more thousands around the world, in locations as diverse as London and Brazil. *(Y2894)*

HOME MARKETS

Forster Green's premises on the corner of Castle Junction and High Street, photographed in 1920 before the building was taken over for Woolworth's new extension. Forster Green's was one of the city's largest tea merchants, although it also dealt in coffee. Its grocery shop advertised not only several brands and qualities of tea, of course, but also O'Neill's 'Reliable' flour, while its street stands are piled high with fruit. *(Y2385)*

Forster Green was as well known for his philanthropy as for his tea. He was involved in a number of good causes, but is remembered with most gratitude for his generosity in making possible new premises and 45 acres of grounds at Fortbreda for the treatment of tuberculosis. In 1907, just before the passing of the Tuberculosis Prevention (Ireland) Act, which compelled county councils to dedicate facilities for the treatment of this scourge, Belfast City Council undertook to maintain thirty-five of the beds at the Forster Green Hospital, thus shouldering responsibility for half of its running costs. In this photograph, Forster Green, in the centre, is presiding at the opening of the new YMCA Reading Room in Wellington Hall, Wellington Place, in the early 1900s. *(Y8566)*

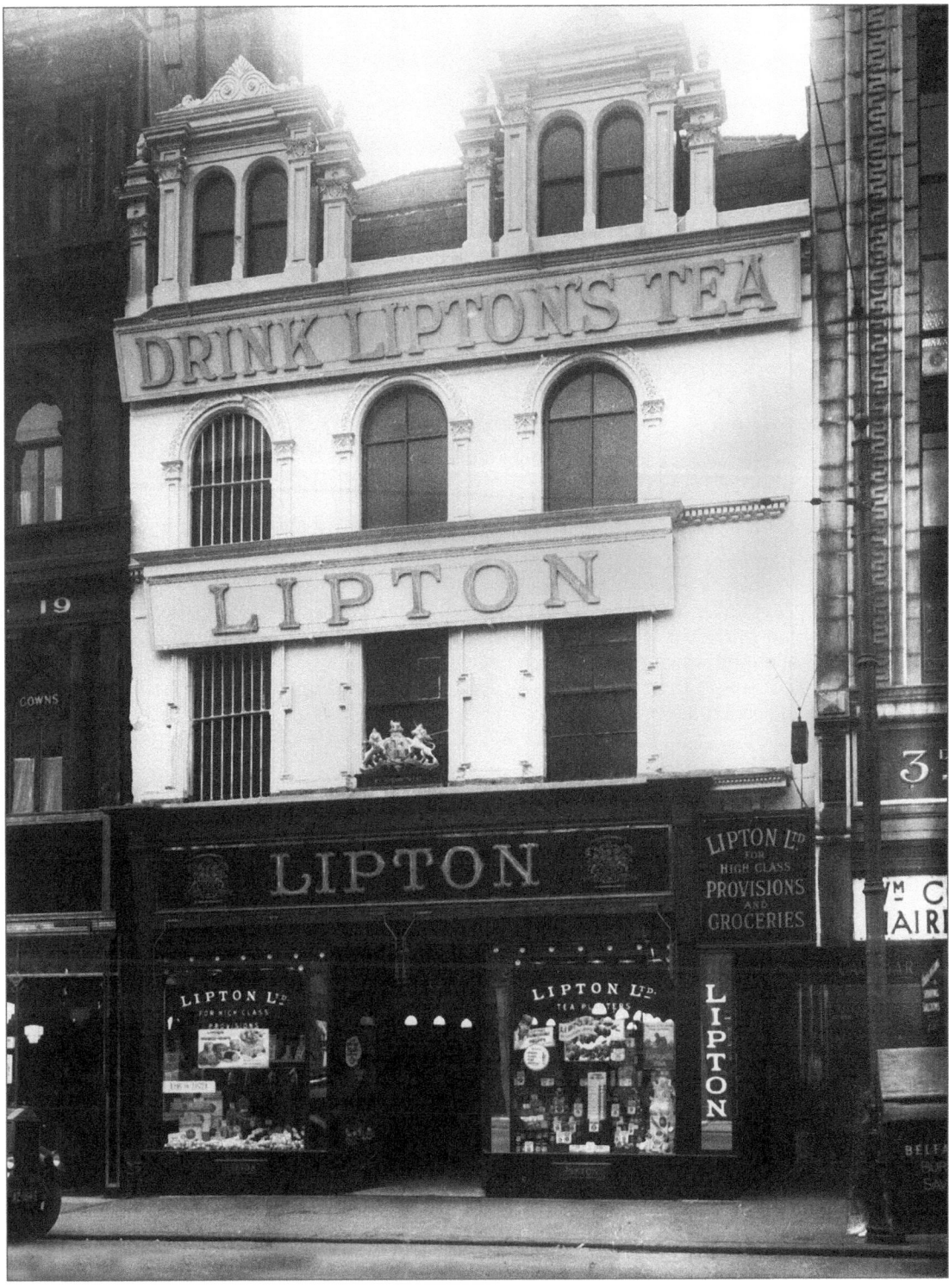

One of several Lipton's tea and grocery shops in Belfast, this one was photographed in 1936 on High Street. Thomas Lipton, founder of the famous chain, was a regular visitor to Belfast. He was a keen sailor and a stalwart member of Royal Ulster Yacht Club, and his beautiful racing yacht, the *Shamrock*, was a familiar sight in Belfast Lough during the 1920s. *(Y2400)*

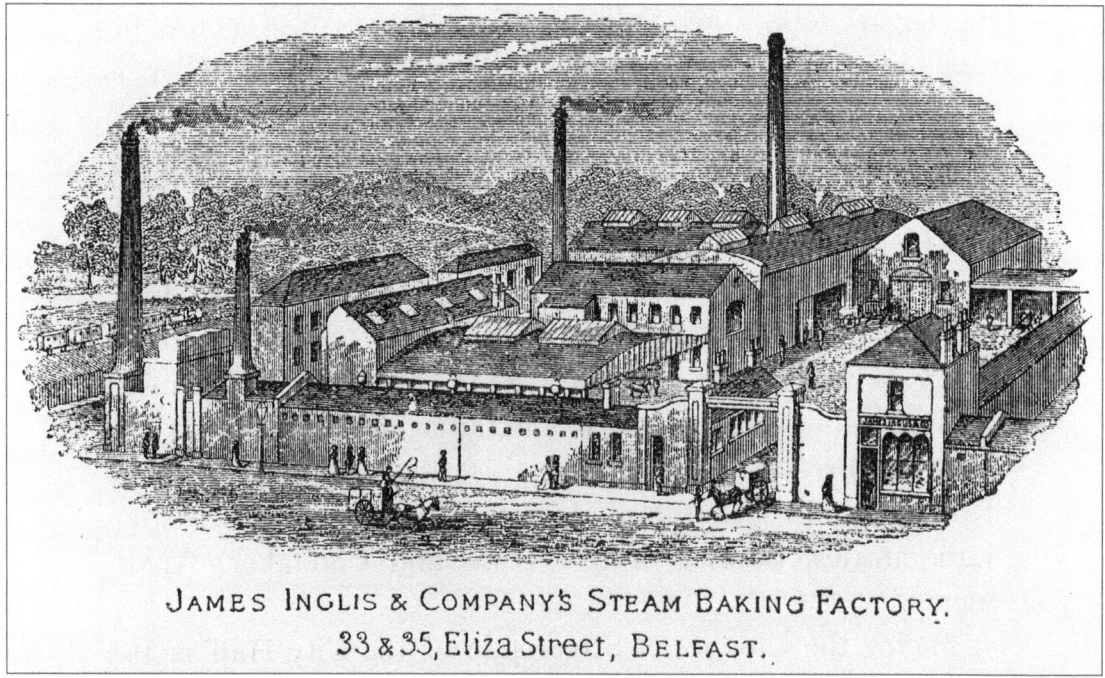

JAMES INGLIS & COMPANY'S STEAM BAKING FACTORY.
33 & 35, Eliza Street, BELFAST.

Inglis's moved to Eliza Street, Belfast, in 1882, having outgrown their old Castle Street bakery. In 1889 they built a five-storey fireproof bakery (not apparent in this letterhead engraving) to the most modern industrial specifications, in which they had such pride and confidence that they invited the public to visit during working hours to see the 'ins and outs' of their modern methods of baking bread in 'one of the most interesting and perfect factories imaginable'. *(Inglis)*

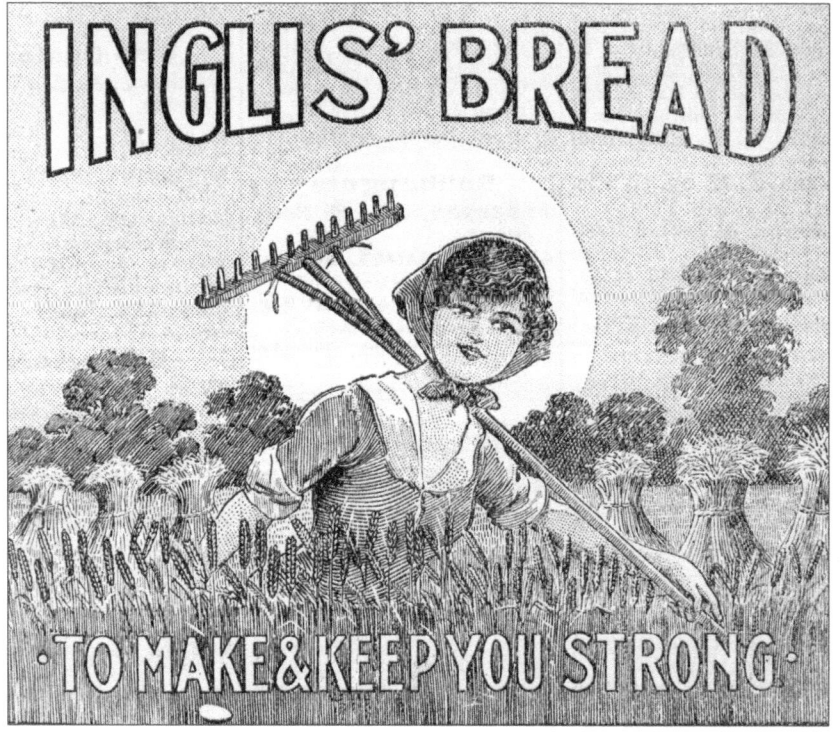

Inglis's bread was advertised and sold throughout the north of Ireland as well as in the city and suburbs where it was made. Its popularity was underpinned by its consistent quality and ensured by its being chosen as the bread served to the Prince and Princess of Wales on their visit to Belfast in 1885 and to Prince Albert Victor when he stayed in the city a few years later. *(Inglis)*

Bernard Hughes's Model Bakery Flour Mills on the Falls Road, from an 1880 advertisement. These mills supplied the Model Bakery's huge factory on Belfast's Springfield Road, producer of the famous 'Barney's Baps' and purveyor of affordable, good quality bread to hungry working families across the north of Ireland. *(Bernard Hughes)*

Rear view of Gibson's Bakery on Soudan Street, January 1937, showing delivery men and their vans. This was one of Belfast's smaller local bakeries, and was obviously flourishing, given the style of its turnout. *(Y3311)*

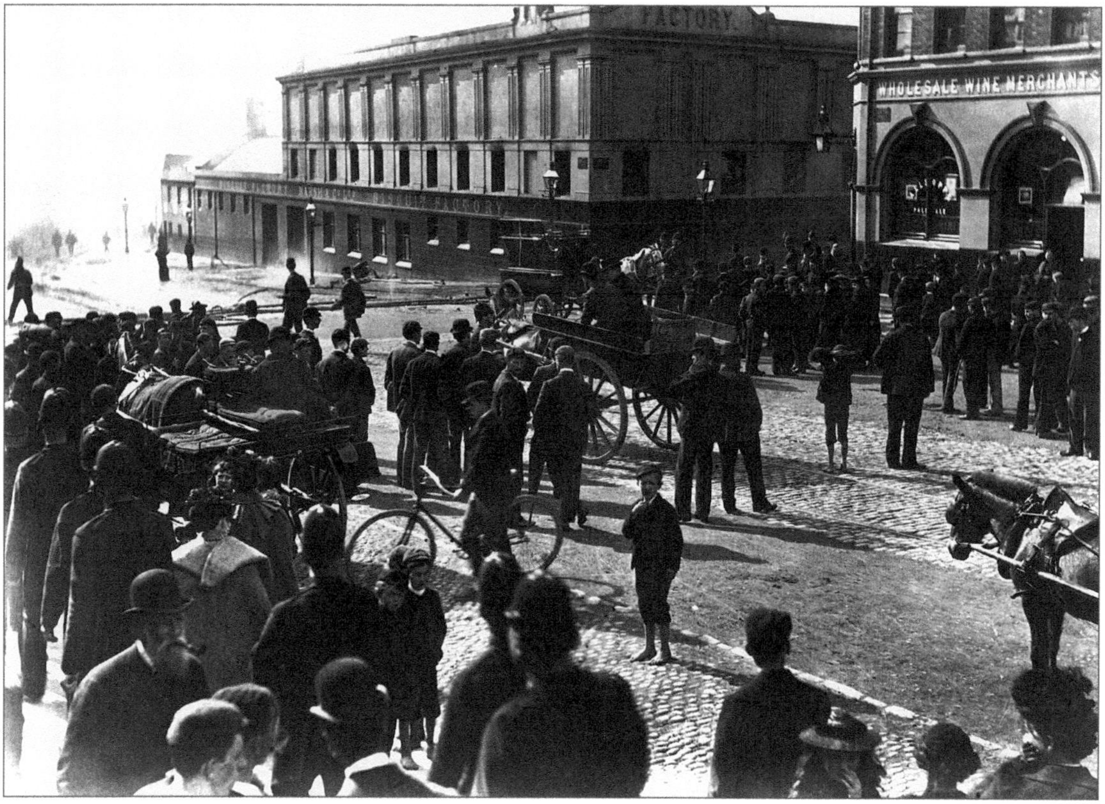
FACTORY
WHOLESALE WINE MERCHANTS

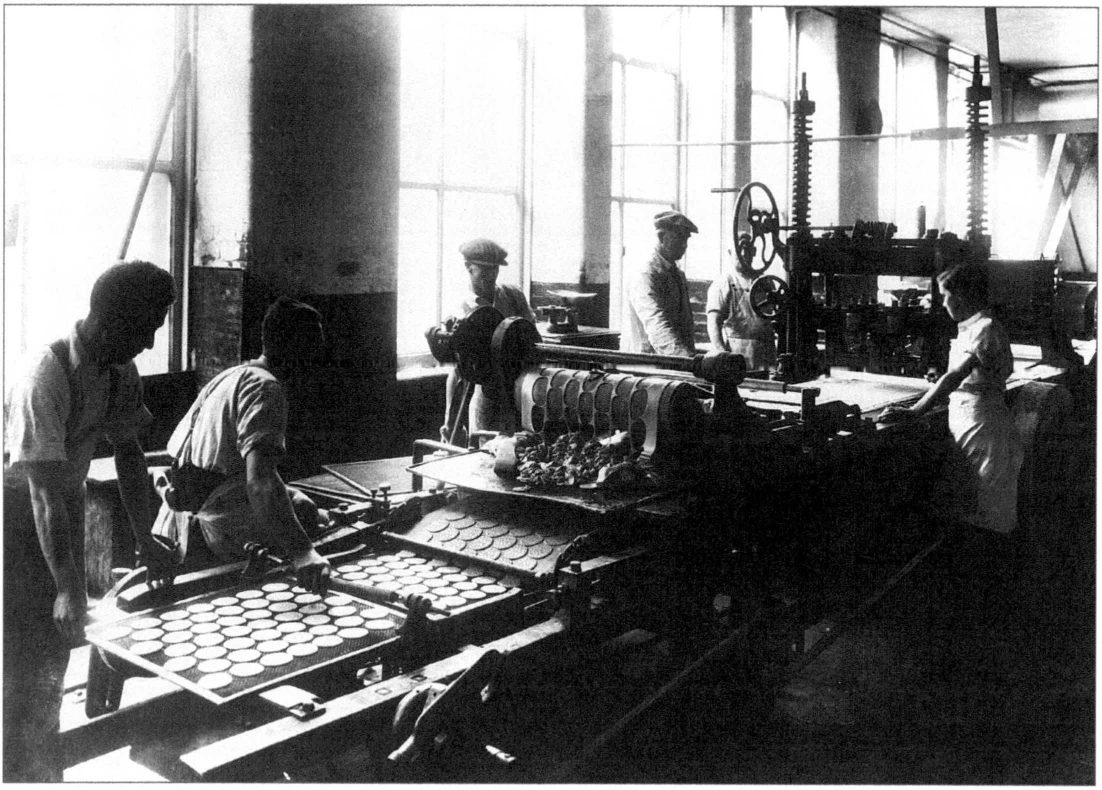

Opposite, top: Belfast Fire Brigade attend a fire at Marsh's Biscuit Factory on Upper Donegall Street, near Carrick Hill, one of the few big employers in this impoverished part of the city. Although the photograph is undated, the horse-drawn fire pump, pulled by the grey horse to the rear of the crowds in the centre background, indicates that this fire occurred before 1910, when the Fire Brigade replaced their horses with motor lorries. *(Y7268)*

Opposite below: Interior of Marsh's new biscuit and cake factory on the Springfield Road in 1931, showing one of the biscuit-cutting machines. Marsh's finally vacated their Donegall Street premises in 1930. This photograph is one of a series commissioned from A.R. Hogg to record the various stages of biscuit-making in the new premises. *(Y1522)*

Right: The Newforge Meals (Irish Food Products) exhibition stand at the Royal Ulster Agricultural Showgrounds in 1932. The Newforge plant, which specialised in processing animal products and by-products, was established at Malone in Belfast in 1929 by Robert Wilson of Barrhead in Scotland. *(H10/52/149)*

One of a series of images taken at Newforge in 1939 by A.R. Hogg, this photograph shows pork being taken off the bone for the manufacture of sausages. Newforge raised its own animals for slaughter and processing before branching out into soft fruit processing from horticultural produce raised on its farms at Portadown. The factory was responsible for much important research into food processing and preservation methods and applications, and was a pioneering force in the field of quick freezing. *(H10/72/36)*

Belfast Co-operative Society began its dairy business in 1913, with a plant capable of dealing with 2,500 gallons of milk per week. This throughput increased tenfold by 1923 and by 1927 had soared to 45,000 gallons per week, an increase in turnover that justified the building of a greatly expanded dairy on Belfast's Ravenhill Road. This photograph is taken from the brochure commemorating the official opening of this most up-to-date facility in 1928 and shows its imposing main entrance. *(Co-op1)*

A general view of the Co-op's milk collection point. The relationship between 'dirty' milk and tuberculosis had long been recognised and challenged through a number of campaigns, most notably in the case of Ireland by the Countess of Aberdeen's 'War on Consumption' which championed pure air, pure food, pure milk and cleanliness as the four weapons used against the disease. The bottle-washing room at the new Ravenhill plant, with its hydraulic scrubbing machines, ensured a degree of cleanliness unknown under older methods of washing, with each bottle receiving an individual treatment of 17 minutes of soaking, scrubbing and rinsing. *(Co-op3)*

Exhibition stands at the Royal Ulster Agricultural Society's showgrounds in May 1930, the first proclaiming Belfast Co-operative Dairy's milk as Belfast's safest. The other stands advertise the work and wares of the Co-operative Wholesale Society, and the International Association of Wholesale Societies. *(H10/52/129)*

One of Belfast Co-operative Dairy's more appealing promotional pieces, extolling the virtues of tuberculin-tested milk for babies and invalids. *(Co-op4)*

Telegraphic Address—"BRADDELL," Belfast.

Pheasant Food.

Season, 1891.

JOSEPH BRADDELL & SON,

21 CASTLE PLACE, BELFAST,

SOLE AGENTS in Ireland for

Chamberlin's Pheasant and Poultry Foods.

These Foods received the Only Award for Game and Poultry Foods from International Jury, Paris Exhibition, 1878. Bronze Medal and Diploma, Mannheim, 1880. Silver Medal, Cleves, 1881. Gold Medal and Diploma of the Societe Belge Avicultura, 1884. Silver Medal, Antwerp, 1885. Honorable Mention, Paris Exhibition, 1889.

REDUCED CASH PRICE LIST.

Aromatic Spanish Meal, ...	per cwt. 26/-	Ground Biscuit Meal, ...	per cwt.	16/-
Meat Greaves for Pheasants, ...	" 26/-	Good Dog Greaves, ...	"	16/-
Arker Excelsior Rice, ...	" 20/-	Superior Dog Greaves, ...	"	20/-
Fowls' Rice, No. 1, ...	" 16/-	Caycar Excelsior, ...	14/- per doz. packets	
Fowls' Rice, No. 2, ...	" 12/-	Aromatic Compound, ...	1/- per doz. packets.	
Canadian Meal, ...	" 18/-	Non-straying Mixture for Pheasants,	2/6 & 5/- ℔ bottle	
Turkeys' Meal, ...	" 20/-	KALYDE, a perfect cure for gapes,	2/- per tin.	

N.B.—2/- per cwt. extra is charged for all Food if Cash is not sent with order.

BAGS and BOXES CHARGED COST PRICE, and are NOT RECEIVED BACK AGAIN.

1 cwt. bag, 1/-; ½ cwt. bag, 8d.

As we receive fresh stocks at intervals during the rearing season, every reliance can be placed on orders being attended to with despatch, and that the **Meal, Greaves, Caycar Excelsior, &c., are quite fresh.** We deliver these goods from our stores here free of any carriage or charge from Norwich to Ireland, thus placing Irish customers on the most favourable terms.

On page 4 will be found copies of a few Testimonials which we have this year received from some of the largest and most successful Pheasant rearers in Ireland.

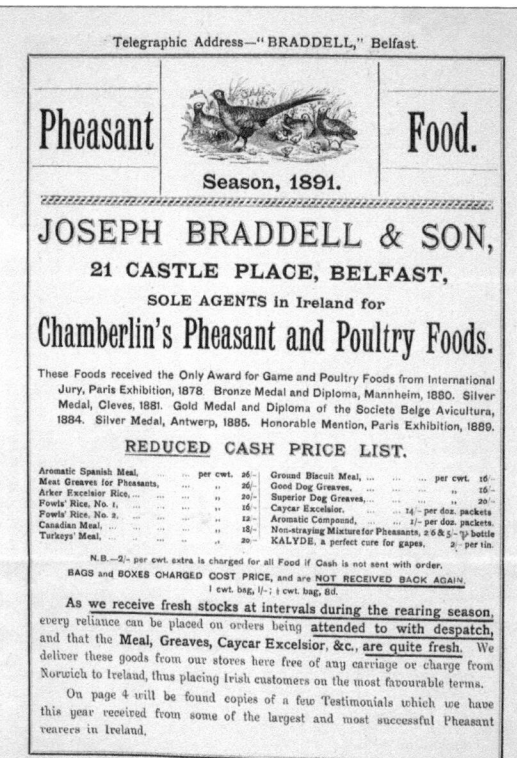

Braddell's of Belfast was best known for the supply of equipment for field sports – fishing rods and, especially, guns and shotguns. However, as this advertisement shows, it also supplied the means of nurturing the very birds that were destined to become the hunter's prey. *(G9DC5192)*

The allotment movement in Belfast was considerably strengthened during the First World War, when a series of competitions was initiated to judge the best garden plot in the city. Here Mr Shirlow, from Stranmillis, stands proudly among his prize-winning cabbages. *(HP10/79/8)*

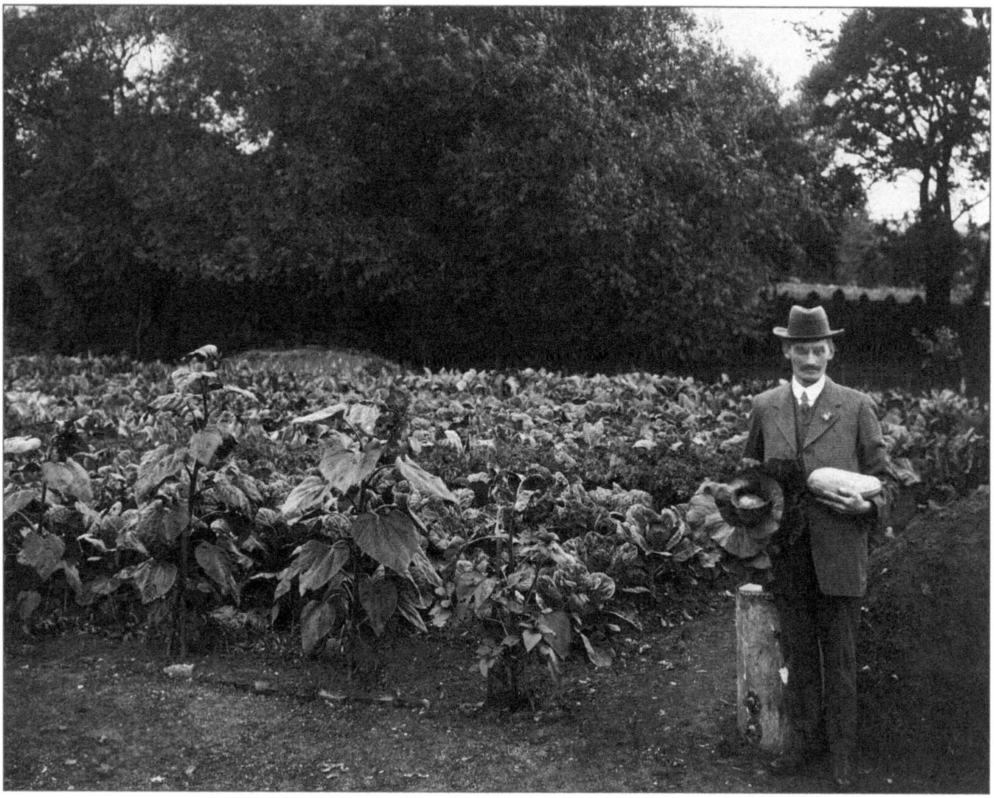

The sound of wooden soles clattering against cobblestones was common in cities and towns across Britain and Ireland in the nineteenth and early twentieth centuries. Many of those worn in Belfast would have been made here, at the Lagan Clog Works on Newforge Lane. *(Y4047)*

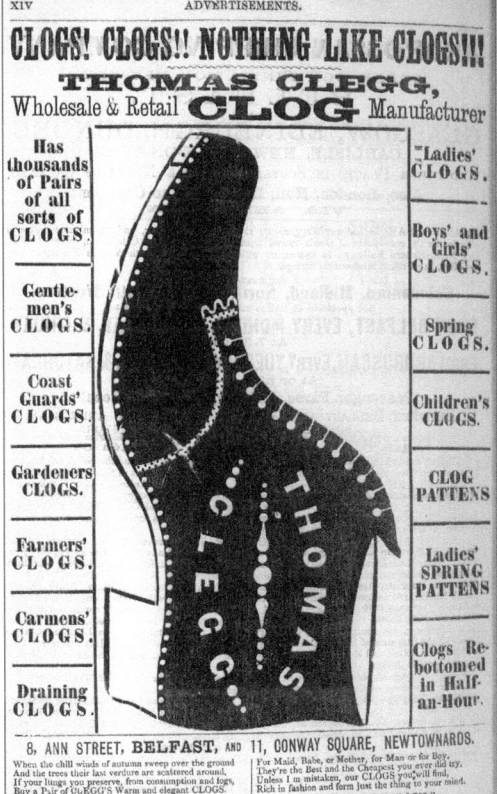

An advertisement for Thomas Clegg's from the 1880 Belfast Street Directory, listing some of the many different types of clogs made by this firm. *(Thomas Clegg)*

The era of off-the-peg clothing (except in the second-hand rag trade patronised by the poor) had yet to come when Hogg took this atmospheric photograph of a band of tailors sitting traditionally cross-legged to work on bespoke suits in the sewing room of W. Marshall, Gents' Outfitter and Tailor, High Street, in 1931. *(H10/21/275)*

The British firm of Thornton's was established in Belfast in the 1850s and gained a reputation throughout Ireland for the quality of its goods. At first they concentrated on waterproof mantles, but became famous for their work with India rubber which, using the newly invented machinery for vulcanisation, they successfully employed across their wide range of sporting, travelling and outdoor wear and equipment; boots and shoes; and mechanical, surgical and domestic manufactures. *(Thorntons)*

THORNTON'S Home of Rubber
all Kinds of
Waterproofs
Made on the Premises
For Cycling, Motor Cycling,
For Fishing, Yachting, Shooting.
AT PRICES TO SUIT EVERYONE.
A Guaranteed Coat for a Lady 21/-
or Gentleman in 4 Shades
24 & 26 DONEGALL PLACE, BELFAST.

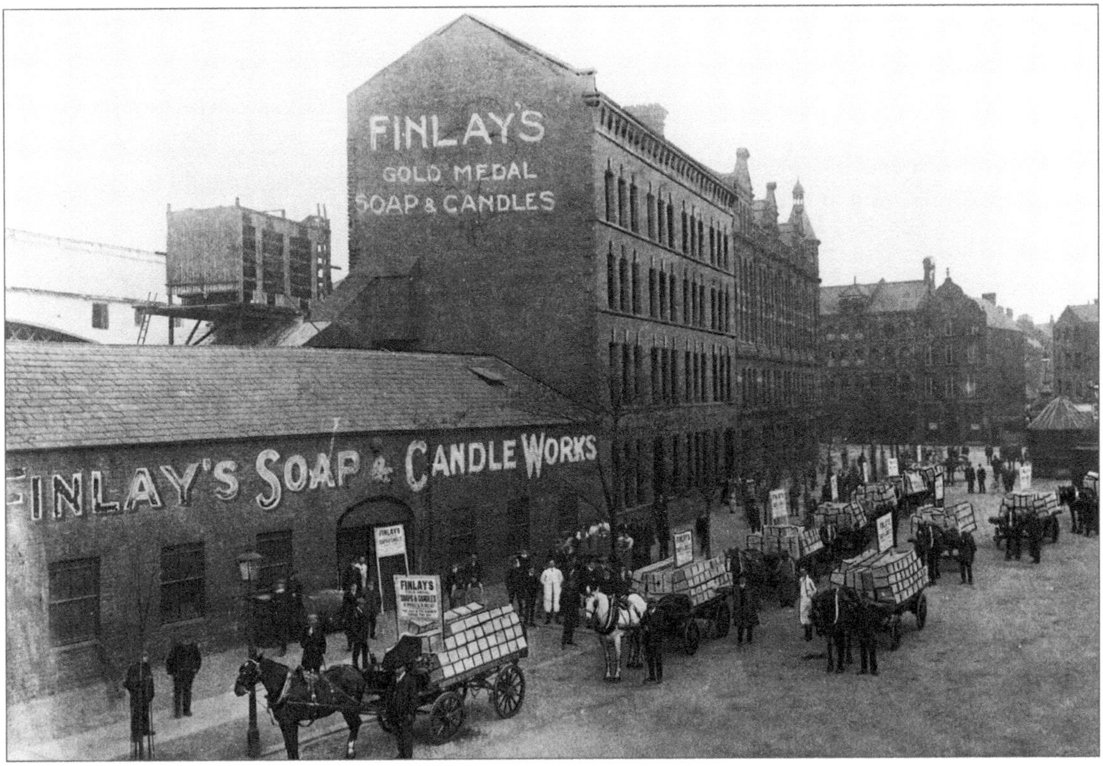

Soap and candle making was a by-industry of the meat and hide trade when Alexander Finlay established his business in Belfast in 1798. In later years, developments in the fields of chemistry and applied science lessened its dependency on animal products and increased both the range and quality of output that could be achieved. A huge variety of Finlay's prize-winning soaps was available, from industrial soaps for bleachers, finishers, laundries and silk and woollen manufacturers to his domestic soap, Silkstone, which pioneered the market in tablet soap. Pure Curd White Soap was unbeatable for washing the finest lawns and muslins; Pine Tar Soap was efficacious against skin complaints; Paraffin Soap offered a strong detergent; while Finlay's Self-Washer Soap was advertised as a great saver of labour and time. The view above shows the firm's Victoria Square premises in 1936. *(Y2712)*

This advertisement, for the laundry bill-cutting reversible shirt solely available at the Belfast firm of John Arnott & Co., appeared in a street directory of 1920. One can only hope that the customers availing themselves of this dubious economy were liberal users of Finlay's soap. Even so, a week spent travelling through and working in the sooty, grimy atmosphere of industrial Belfast must have left its imprint. *(AD8)*

Advertisement for the Shankhill Shrouding Warehouse in an 1896 street directory, one of only two such outfitters listed in Belfast, along with eight undertaking firms. *(AD5)*

4

Street Level

A dapper assistant strikes a confident pose at the doorway of James's Boys', Youths' and Gents' Select Clothing Hall in Lombard Street, *c.* 1909. Note the column of sailor suits descending on the inner side of the right-hand window. *(Y8573)*

The premises of Samuel Hogg's 'The Peoples' Tea & Coffee Warehouse', 6–8 Shankhill Road. Samuel Hogg was the uncle of the Belfast photographer A.R. Hogg, who took this picture in about 1920 and who is responsible for very many of the other images of people at work featured in this volume. Note the coalman and his horse posing at the left-hand side, close to a sign advertising the best English and Scotch [sic] coals, ex-ship or yard, and the impressive array of flitches of bacon and hams festooned around the shop window. (Y3935)

W.R. Rangecroft's shop at 229 Antrim Road, photographed in April 1931 under 'exclusively new management', as the sign in the window on the right reads. The delivery boy with his bicycle stands proudly on the left looking eager to impress his new boss. (Y3319)

One of the Belfast branches of the Dewhurst chain of butchers, at 49 Ann Street, 1936. It was presumably springtime, as the jugs of fresh irises in the window suggest. *(Y1674)*

More flowers, this time in the gloriously illuminated windows of Frank E. Smith & Co., Florists, of 11 Wellington Place. *(HP10/21)*

The basement display at R. Hogg's famous shop in Donegall Square, Belfast, photographed in 1936 advertising 'one thousand and one things for smaller gifts, bridge prizes and the adornment of your home' and tea services ranging in price from 8s 11d to £40! *(Y2809)*

Photographed while the structural alterations that created the new basement shown above were being completed, here the staff of Hogg's are pictured before embarking on the bus which took them on a summer outing in July 1935. *(Y2092)*

Dobbin's City Stores in North Street, beside the Alhambra 'Theatre of Varieties'. A surprising range of goods handled is indicated in this photograph, which includes notices for Kodak film, for compounding prescriptions and for tea. Note the liveried young man standing outside the entrance. *(Y2498)*

The staff of Dobbin's, photographed in 1907. *(Y4653)*

Women eagerly examine provisions displayed in the covered stall outside T.W. Henning's butcher's shop at 239 Antrim Road in April 1934. Note the chickens hanging under the awning. *(Y3321)*

Street vegetable trader sheltering from the sun in the Markets area of Belfast, *c.* 1905. *(Y8567)*

Shops on Cromac Street from a photograph taken in 1915: from right to left, McNulty's Fruiterers; Magee's Kitchenware and China; and McKay & Co.'s Drapers. The extent of street-level activity depicted here, with doorways thronged by passers-by and goods cascading on to pavements, is typical of small shopping localities in towns and cities across Ireland at the beginning of the twentieth century. *(Y3033)*

One of Belfast's best-known and most-missed shopping heavens is Rebecca Gilmore's household effects and furniture shop in Smithfield Market, the doorway flanked by what appears to be a roll of sheepskin, and, beside it, the Working Men's Clothing Company – the Cheapest House in the City. The long stick held by the boy standing to the right of the doorway would have been used to unhook the suits and coats displayed on high when the shop closed for the night. *(Y2669)*

The exterior of Johnston's famous umbrella shop at 31 High Street, Belfast, photographed in 1935 before the business moved to premises in Ann Street. Beside it at no. 29 was the studio of the photographer William Abernethy, established in 1886 and responsible for taking many fine portraits of the great and the good of the city. *(Y2350)*

The Co-op boot shop at 120 Mount-pottinger Road, *c.* 1910. *(Belfast Co-op)*

The hat department at Anderson & McAuley's department store in Royal Avenue. One wonders whether the girl on the right looking into the camera is a customer, or a model for the more mature ladies looking on. *(Y33335)*

A busy scene in Belfast's North Street, showing Thomas Campbell's brush factory and showroom and, beside it, the 'Hustler' boot and shoe store, which was having a clearance sale before moving premises. On its gable wall is a poster of an elegant gentleman proclaiming, 'I sell boots here', and above it the inspired slogan, 'Take these boots off our hands and put them on your feet!' *(Y2497)*

New premises for Austin Reed's Gentlemen's Outfitters in Donegall Place, 1930. The new premises straddled Belfast's Queen's Arcade, home to fine clothing, millinery and dressmaking outlets. The white-coated man holding the placard is inviting passers-by to partake of the hospitality of the Queen's Café – Bar and Restaurant. *(Y1916)*

Sammy Justice's stand at the radio exhibition in The Plaza Ballroom on Chichester Street in September 1936. The firm operated from premises on Donegall Road, and boasted a fine range of brands and models. *(Y1755)*

A window display at the Belfast Corporation Electricity Showroom in Wellington Place, photographed in November 1937, a pertinent time of year to be advertising the benefits of investing in 'the HomeSun', a scary-looking device of some size and complexity. *(Y2757)*

The Ideal Trading Stamp Co. showrooms on Victoria Square, photographed in April 1932. The wrappers of products sold under the Ideal brand, such as soap, tea and tinned fruit and fish, could be exchanged for gifts chosen from offices such as these. The company also had branches in Dublin, various cities in Scotland, the north of England and London. *(Y2720)*

5

At Your Service

Hotel attendants and restaurant staff at Belfast's Grand Central Hotel pose for their photograph on 30 April 1936. *(Y2644)*

The luxurious dining room of Belfast YMCA's Café Royal in Wellington Place, with its cheerful serving staff, photographed in April 1933. *(Y2779)*

A waiter and bellboy at the Belgravia House Hotel on Ulsterville Avenue pose in the dining room on 17 May 1932. *(Y3709)*

Advertisement for the Imperial Hotel, Donegall Place, in 1863, promising 'a first-class commercial and family hotel combining English comfort with Parisian elegance'; a coffee room for gentlemen; drawing rooms, each with a piano; the best commercial room in the United Kingdom; show rooms; livery stables; baths; and a café and restaurant. *(Imperial Hotel)*

The same hotel nearly fifty years later. Note how the ground floor has been given over to shops, and how the building has been extended upwards to provide two additional floors of rooms. *(Y1948)*

In the 1930s Belfast supported eighteen commercial laundries, taking washing from businesses and private customers. Here, drivers from the Globe Laundry and Dyeworks with premises at Willowbank on the Falls Road show off its fleet of newly acquired motor vans. *(Y3405)*

Staff of the Devonshire Laundry on the Ravenhill Road, photographed on 10 April 1931. *(Y3816)*

The Devonshire's fleet of horse-drawn carts, each with driver and side-kick, also photographed on 10 April 1931. Behind can be seen some of the motor vans that were also used to collect and deliver laundry. *(Y3813)*

Women workers ironing shirts at the Devonshire Laundry in February 1931. Note the makeshift work stands, the mountains of collar-less shirts and the rows of pin-ups of film stars lining the wall in the background. *(Y3817)*

Some big houses had no need of the commercial laundries, as this image of a Belfast washerwoman using a washboard at her sink indicates, *c.* 1905. Note the double taps, evidence of both hot and cold running water, and the woman's shawl hanging behind her. *(Y8598)*

Above: No pictures of film stars in the pressing and ironing room at the Monarch Laundry when it was photographed in May 1936, just piles of sheets and shirts. Note the various types of industrial irons in use, and how young some of the girls working them appear to be. *(Y3295)*

Right: Advertisement for W.G. Hanna, sole agent for the time- and labour-saving patent 'Home' washer machine. One of the testimonials advertised was from a Victorian gentleman, not the type of person traditionally expected to have much familiarity with the efficiency or otherwise of a washing machine. *(Wringer)*

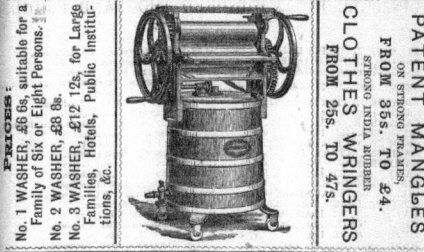

Left: Not everyone who worked in the laundries was intimately involved with processing dirty linens, as this photograph of women working in the offices of the Monarch Laundry in 1936 shows. Note the woman using a typewriter on the left, whose seat has been elevated a goodly distance by the addition of some books. This was a temporary solution to the problem of working seated at a desk designed to be used by a man standing, and a nice illustration of the relatively late arrival of women to office work. *(H10/33/4)*

Female student teachers from the Scientific Cookery Department at the Municipal College of Technology on College Square East, photographed with their instructor in May 1930. *(Y1818)*

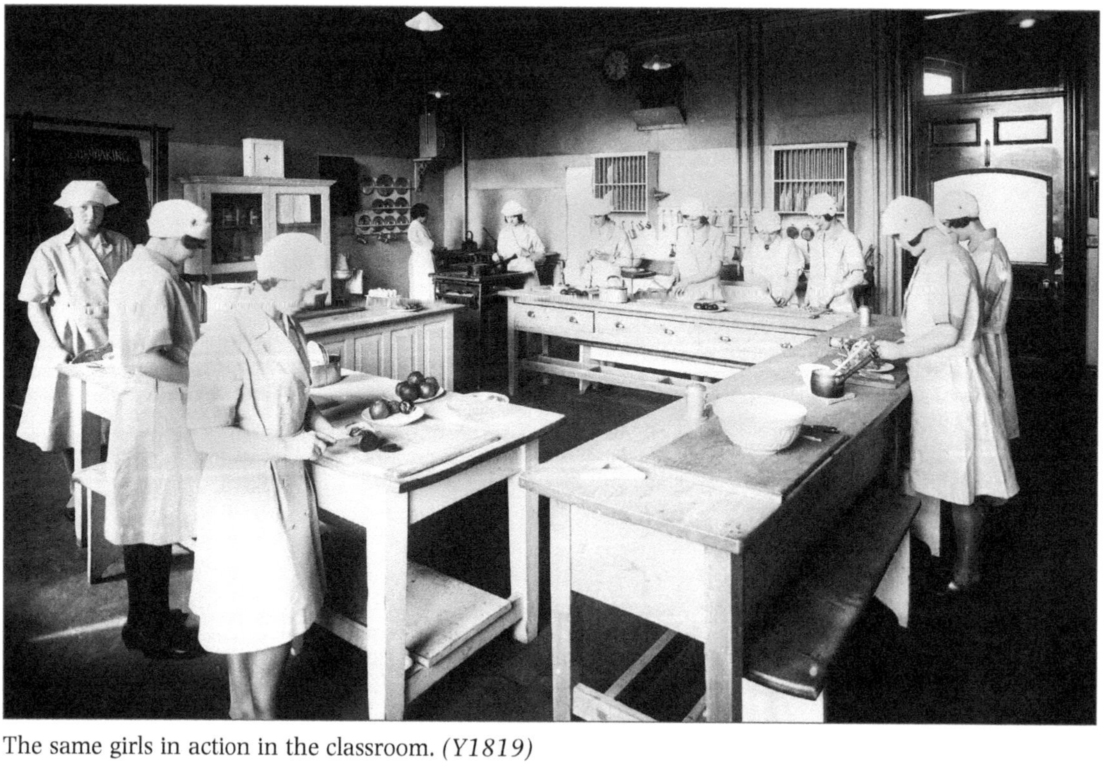

The same girls in action in the classroom. *(Y1819)*

A marvellously contrived photograph of a plumbing class at the College of Technology, *c.* 1910, with boys examining a piping system from every conceivable angle. *(HB65)*

Less stereotypically, perhaps, this photograph shows female chemistry students at the Municipal College of Technology working on experiments in the chemistry laboratory in May 1930. Note, however, that classes were still segregated along lines of gender. *(Y1806)*

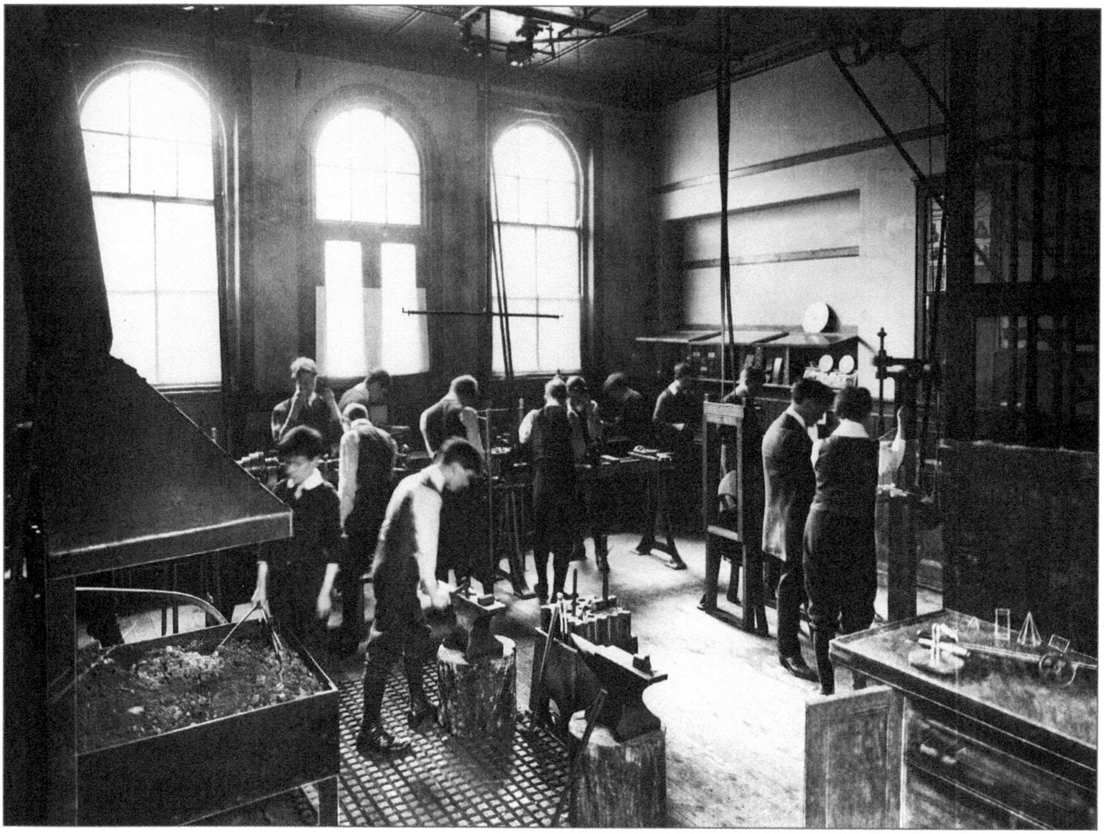

A pre-apprenticeship metalwork class at the Christian Brothers Trade Preparatory School at Hardinge Street in March 1912. *(W10/35/10)*

This Indenture MADE the First day of November in the Year of our Lord One Thousand Eight Hundred and forty nine BETWEEN Christopher Dickson of Lagan Village in the County of Down of the one part, AND William Coates and John Young of Ballym[illegible] in the County of Down of the other part, WITNESSETH, that the said Christopher Dickson by and with the approbation and consent of his father Wm Dickson of Ballymacarrett in the County of Down doth put himself Apprentice to the said William Coates and John Young Iron founders to learn the art and Trade of A smith and with them after the manner of an Apprentice to dwell and serve from the First day of November One thousand eight hundred and forty nine for and during the full term and space of Seven Years from thence next ensuing, to be fully complete and ended. DURING which term, the said Apprentice his said Masters faithfully shall serve, their secrets keep, their lawful commands every where gladly do: he shall do no damage to his said Masters in their Goods, Chattels, or Estate, or know or procure any to be done by others; but, when he shall know, or have any reason to suspect any such being intended, he shall forthwith give warning to his said Masters of the same: he shall not waste the Goods of his said Masters, or give or lend them unlawfully to any: he shall not commit fornication, or contract matrimony, within the said term; hurt to his said Masters in their person or family, he shall not do, cause, or procure to be done of others: he shall not play at cards, dice, or any unlawful game, with his own or others' goods, whereby his said Masters may have loss, during the said term. Without license of his said Masters he shall neither buy nor sell: he shall not frequent taverns, ale-

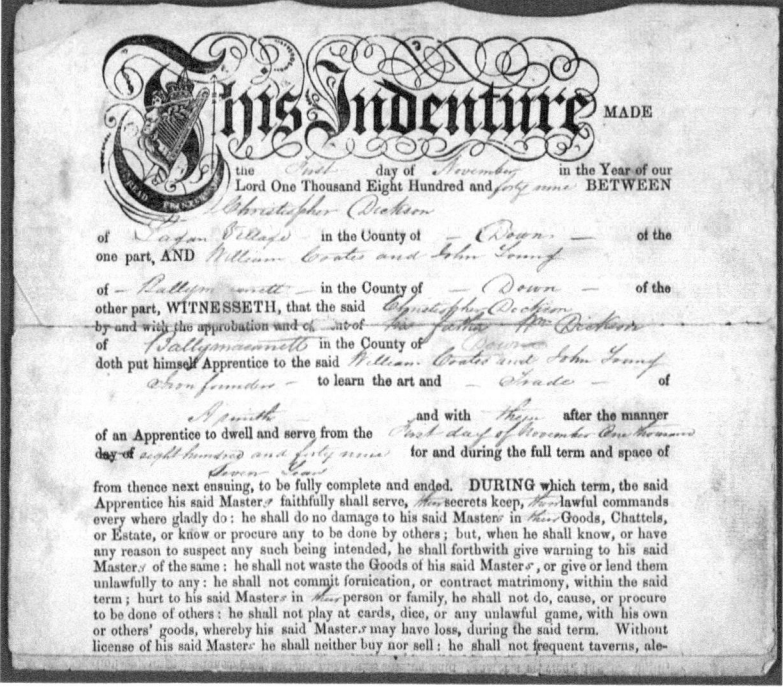

Copy of the opening paragraphs of an indenture entered into on 1 November 1849 between Christopher Dickson and William Coates and John Young, iron founders of Ballymacarrett, whereby Christopher, with the consent of his father William, put himself forward as an apprentice for seven years to learn the trade of a smith. *(DSC1675)*

Bootmaking class, Balmoral Industrial School, Belfast, *c.* 1910. The Balmoral school was the only one in Ireland for Protestant boys and was certified to take up to 400 pupils. The object of the industrial schools was to rescue orphaned, homeless and destitute boys from the perils and temptations of street life and teach them useful trades. *(Y8581)*

At least life at Balmoral Industrial School was lived on dry land. This rare image shows the training ship *Grampian* moored in Belfast Lough before she was sold for breaking in 1899 and her charges transferred to Balmoral. Established in 1872 under the Industrial Schools (Ireland) Act of 1868, the ship acted as a boarding school for homeless and destitute boys, who were trained up to enter a trade or to join the merchant marine. *(Y4098)*

Members of Belfast City Mission, with the Reverend Mr Montgomery in the centre. Not to be confused with Belfast Central Mission, which operated under the auspices of Methodism, Belfast City Mission was aligned with the city's Presbyterian Church. Its aim, however, was much the same – to bring succour and shelter as well as the gospel and godliness to the city's poor and disadvantaged. *(Y4645)*

Belfast's numerous missions offered recreational and leisure opportunities to those they served, as well as physical and spiritual support. This photograph shows members of the Kingham Mission to the Deaf and Dumb partaking of a variety of board games at its headquarters in Botanic Avenue in August 1939. *(Y2999)*

A.R. Hogg's masterful photograph of Joseph Forde weaving coarse matting in the Workshops for the Industrious Blind in Lawnbrook Avenue in 1937. The image was published in the *Radio Times* as part of a national appeal for the blind. *(H10/69/31)*

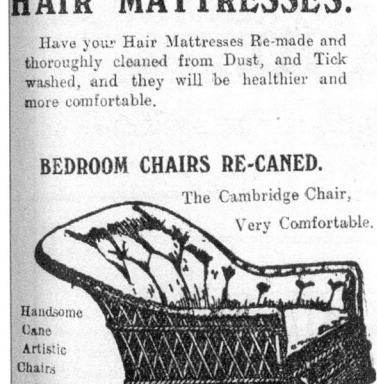

An advertisement for some of the other products manufactured at the Workshops for the Blind and sold through their retail outlet on Royal Avenue. *(Hair Mattresses)*

SMOKING CONCERT AUCTION - In aid of Princess Mary's Sailors & Soldiers Christmas Fund. 4th Dec. 1914. Organized by W.J. McCOY & SONS, LTD BELFAST
J.P. McCOY, F.A.I. in the Rostrum.
BERNARD J. McCOY, Co-Director.

A smoking concert at which, indeed, many of the members of the party are smoking – was it obligatory? *(Y4668)*

The executive of W.J. McCoy, photographed in 1905 with one of the machines they stored in their Smithfield warehouses. Mr J.P. McCoy, Master of Ceremonies in the auction pictured above, is on the far left. *(Y2672)*

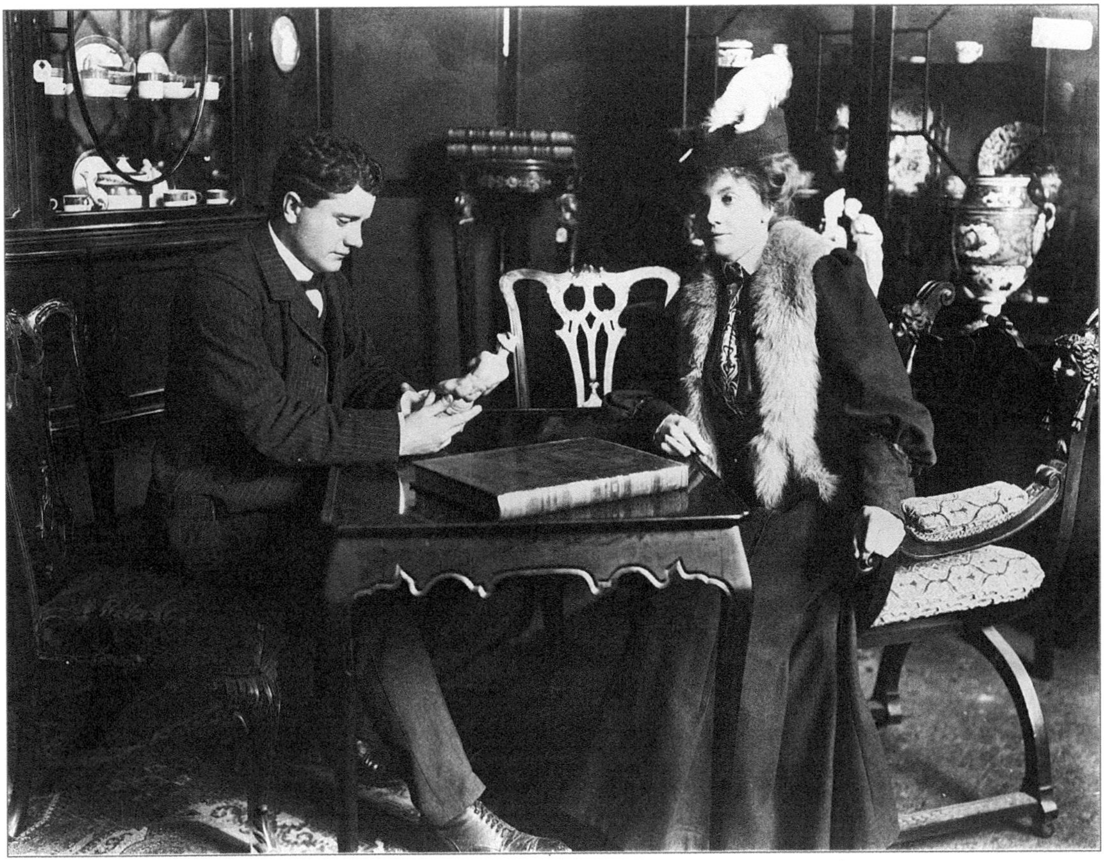

W.J. McCoy's of Smithfield at work as one of their specialists examines an ornament in their antiques department for a smartly dressed customer in 1905. *(Y2674)*

Furniture Warehouse, Auction Mart, Offices, and Machinery Stores.

Telephone No. 789. Established 1860.

Dealers in High-Class Second-Hand Furniture · Antiques, Works of Art, Billiard Tables · Office Furniture · Safes · &c &c

Machinery Dealers and General Brokers · Auctioneers & Valuers · Entire Contents of Works Mills &c Purchased.

84 to 86, Smithfield, Belfast, Aug. 25th 1909

Mr W Mann Esq

Bought of 3 The Mall Armagh

W. J. McCoy & Sons, Limited.

All goods invoiced at nett prices.

2 Carved walnut chairs in R. damask	1	15 ·
1 Rosewood easy - in tapestry	1	5 ·
Mahy. dressing glass	1	15
	£4	15
By Cheque	£4	15

For W. J. McCoy & Sons, Limited. ONE PENNY

With thanks 25/8/09

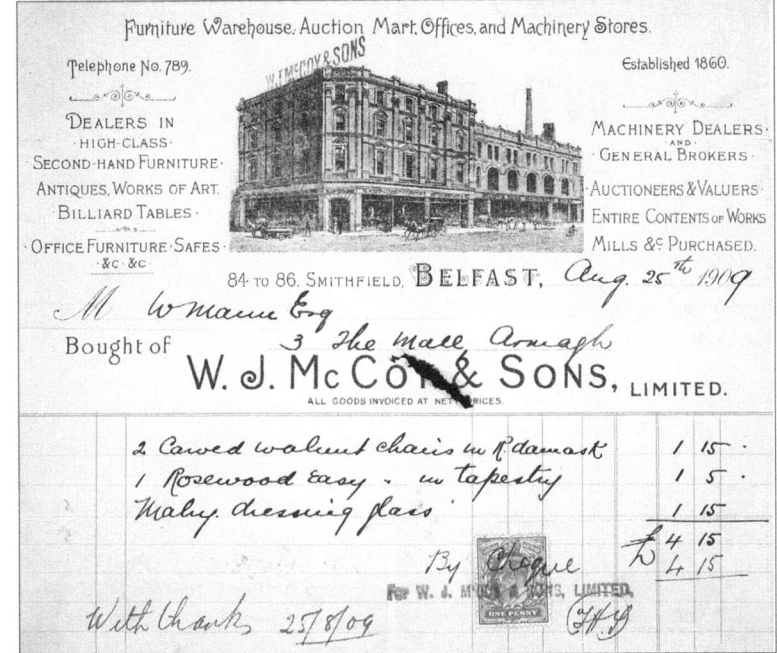

A W.J. McCoy's billhead from 1909, carrying an engraving of their extensive premises and a list of the services and facilities they provided. An elegant Armagh address surely deserved elegant furniture, and at what appears to be a very elegant price! *(G9DC5202)*

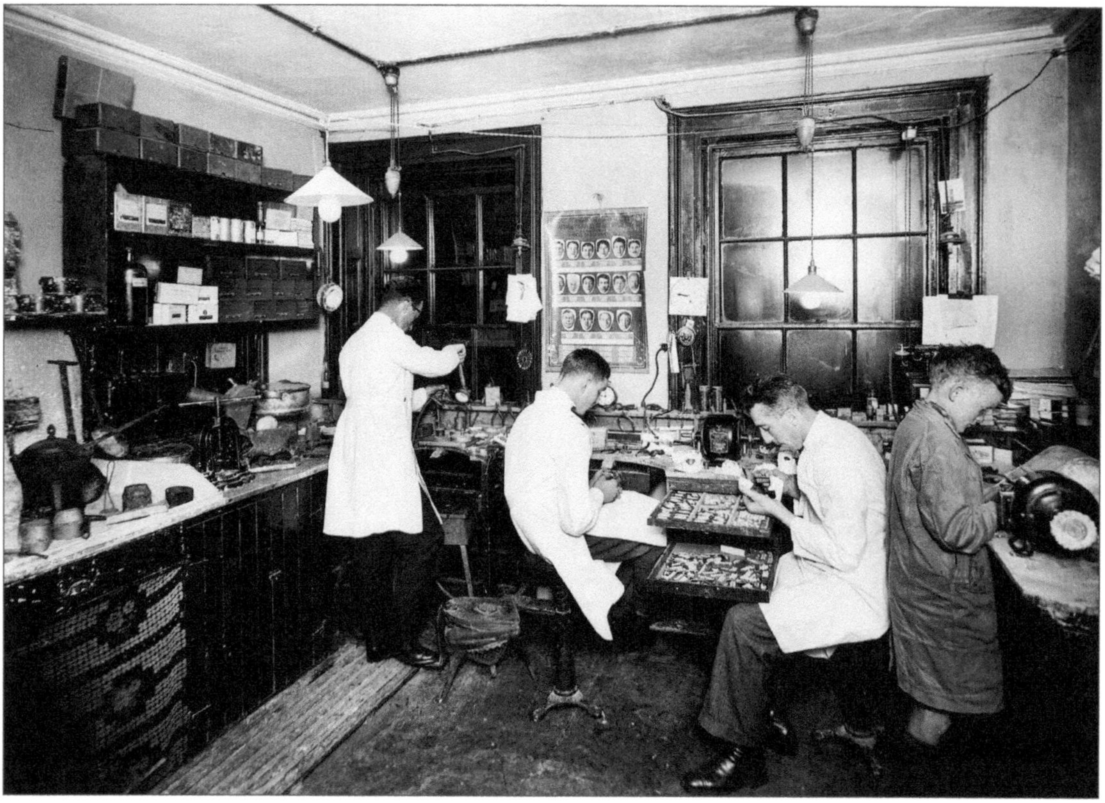

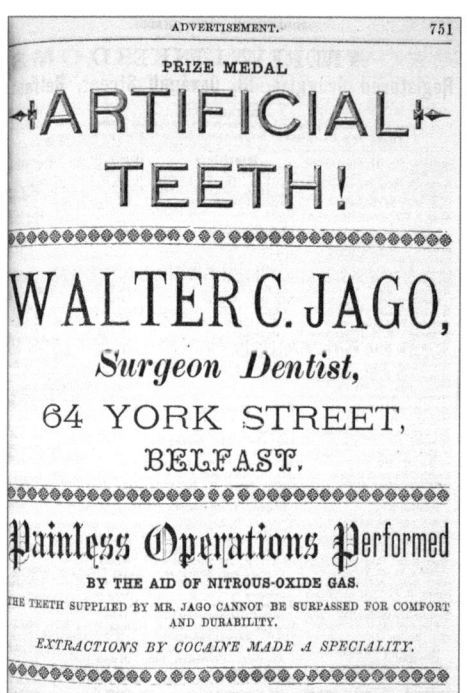

Dental mechanics making false teeth at McCallister's, Wellington Place, in September 1929. Note the poster on the wall between the windows classifying different shapes of face and jaw. The young apprentice on the right with short trousers and a face full of freckles must have been straight from school. *(Y2796)*

Left: This advertisement, published in 1892, gives some idea of the cost and nature of dental treatment in Belfast at the turn of the century. Notice what a long day Mr Jago worked! *(Jago)*

Opposite: This picture of Mr Jago's York Street premises was sent as a postcard to a lady in Craigavad, *c.* 1900. Perhaps it was a hint that she should get her teeth fixed? *(10/21/253)*

A technician grinding spectacle lenses in Harris Rundle's optician's shop in Donegall Place, November 1931. *(Y1888)*

The X-Ray Department at Queen's University, photographed in October 1905. *(H10/79/85)*

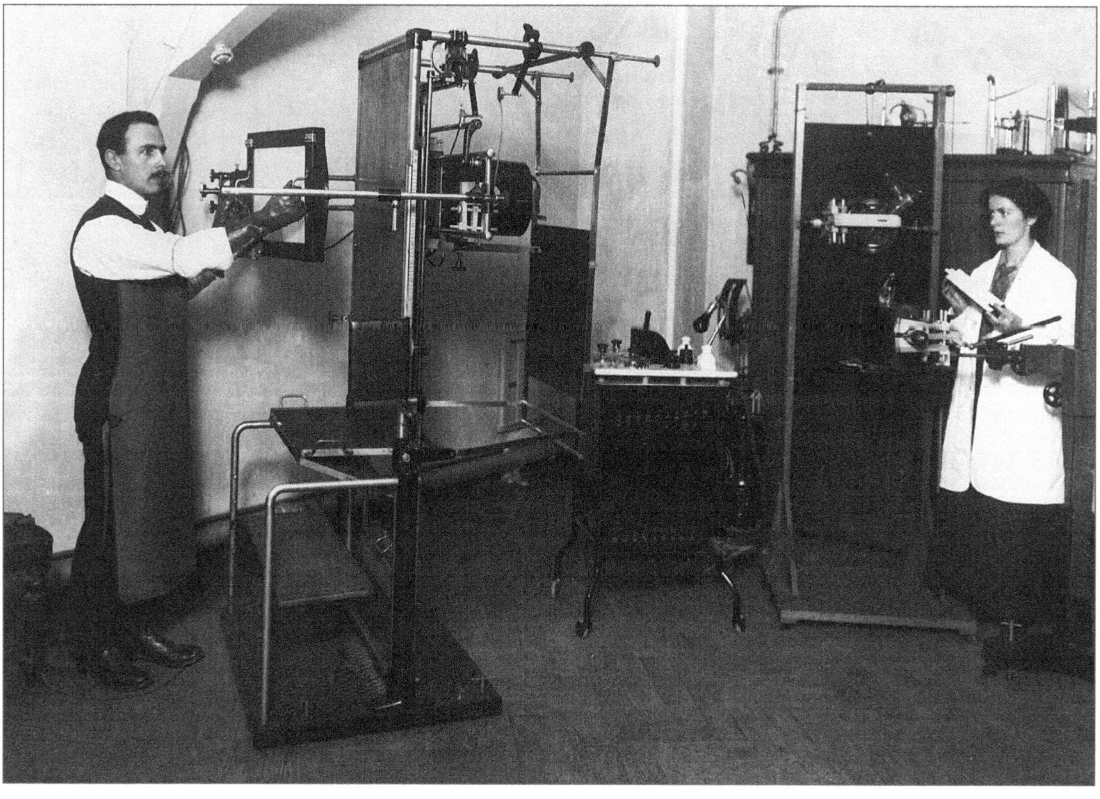

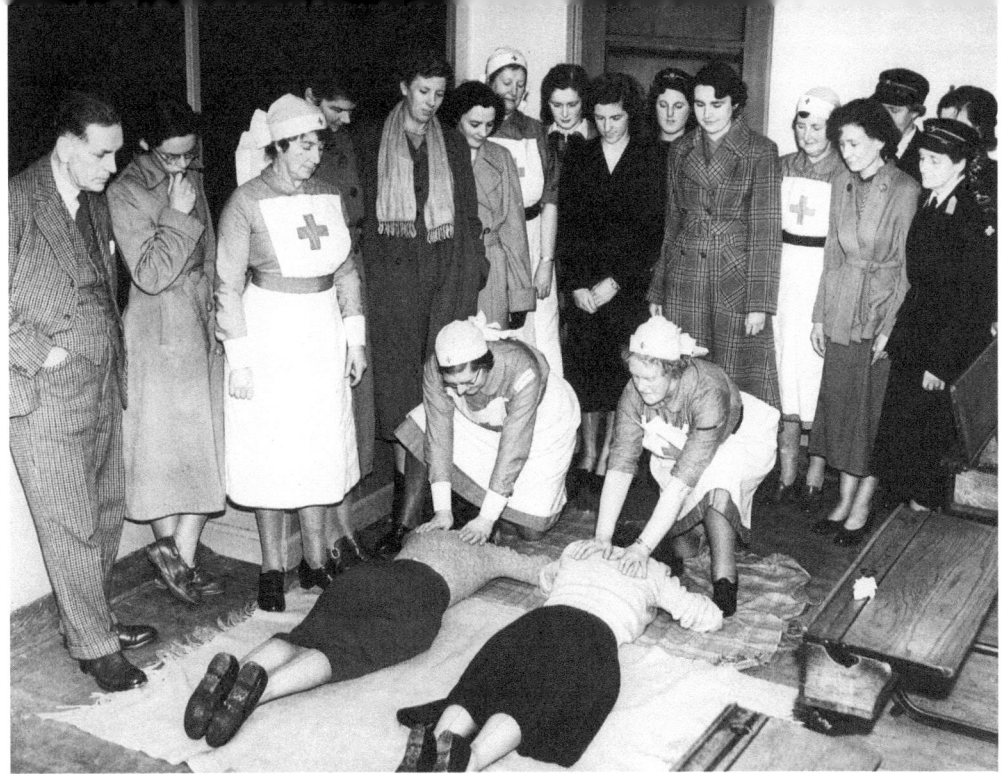

Undated, but presumably from the late 1930s or early 1940s, this photograph shows new recruits of the Hospital Service Reserve watching Mrs U. Spry, County Director (Belfast), British Red Cross Society, and Mrs J. Heanen, Quartermaster, 54 Detachment, demonstrate the Holger-Nelson method of artificial respiration at McQuiston School in Belfast. *(PS18)*

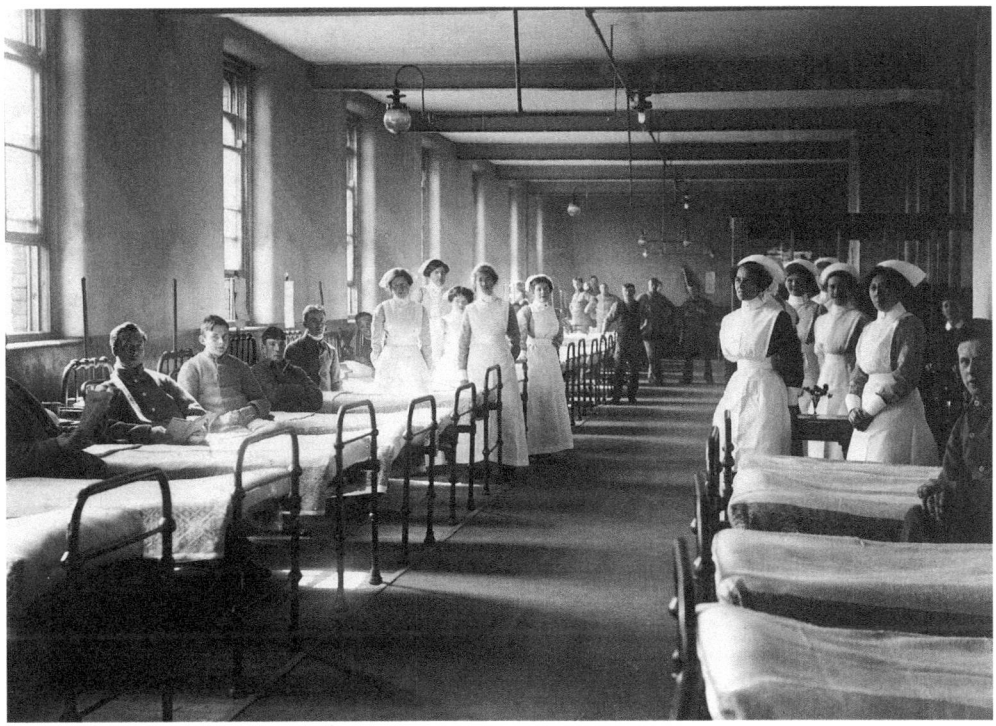

The legendary Miss Gault casts a watchful eye over her ward in Belfast Union Infirmary (City Hospital) in 1917. *(PS20)*

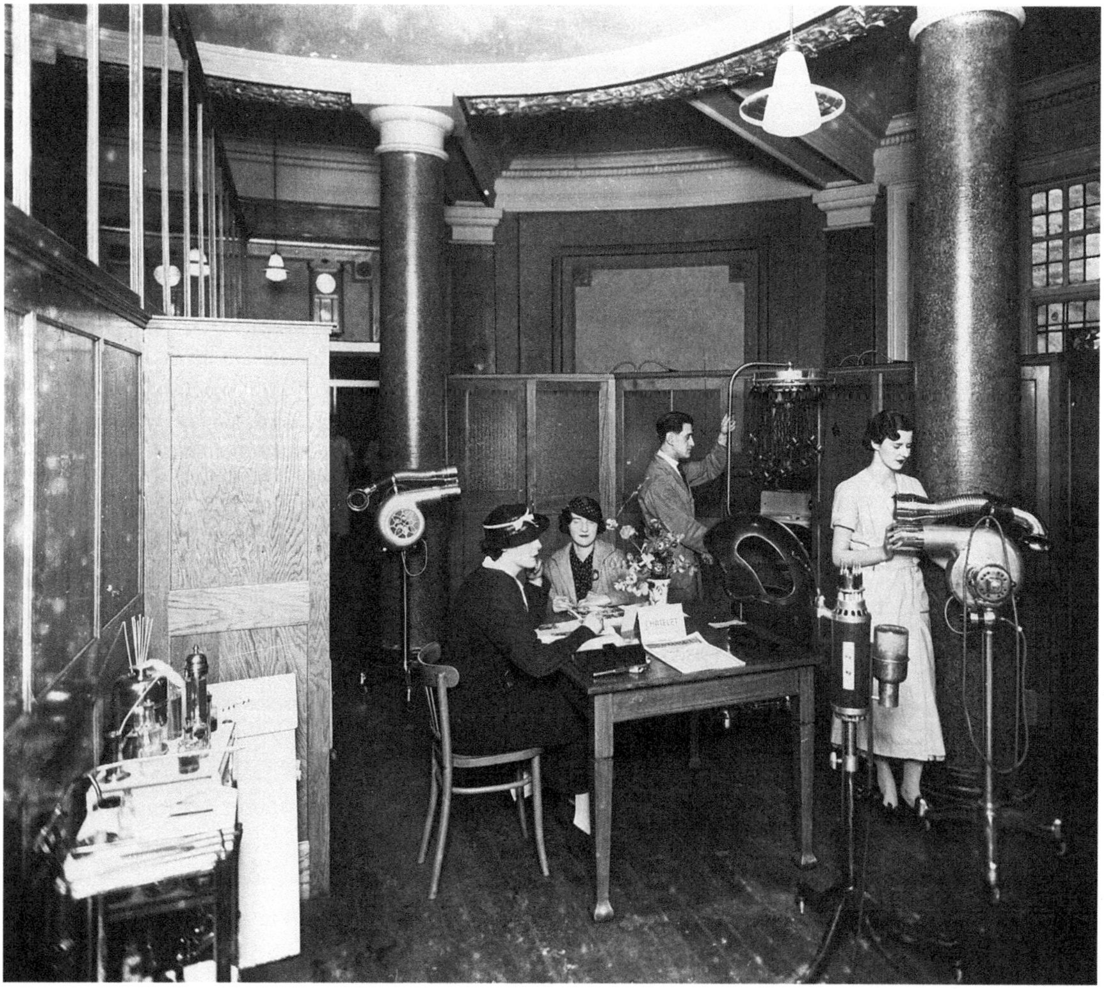

Eliza Lynch sitting at her big Irish spinning wheel at the Irish Exhibition organised by the Belfast Industrial Development Association in the Ulster Hall on Bedford Street, 1912. In her hands she holds a pair of carders, used to separate sections of the woolly fleece into fine strands for spinning into yarn. In the background is a Dutch, or Castle, wheel, set up with a flax distaff to spin linen yarn. *(Y2964)*

Opposite, above: This detail of a larger photograph shows a demonstration of the McDonald System of Hair Waving (using the fearsome-looking device suspended over the head of the seated woman in the centre) at the Carlton Restaurant in Donegall Place, 1932. *(Y1912)*

Opposite, below: The interior of M. Mallan's hairdressing salon, Castle Arcade, in June 1935, showing the ladies' waiting room and some of the equipment used, including the McDonald System described above. *(Y1724)*

Crowds entering the Belfast Industrial Development Association's Irish Exhibition at its Queen Street offices in August 1911. *(Y2114)*

Ulster Industries Development Association posters, photographed somewhere in Belfast in 1934, exhorting passers-by to buy goods produced at home or within the Empire. This and the above photograph in juxtaposition neatly encapsulate the profound changes in the nature and direction of Irish trade and production networks following the partition of the country in 1922. *(Y4224)*

In 1907 the Liverpool-Irish-born James Larkin was sent to Belfast as Union Organiser by James Sexton of the National Union of Dock Labourers. So effective was he in uniting their workers that the employers fought back, seeking to break the new union by locking out members and thus provoking the Belfast Dockers' and Carters' Strike, which lasted from May to November 1907 and succeeded in closing many of the city's industries. Here, a cartload of grain is being escorted through the streets of Belfast by a military escort, one of many such heavily protected services which were delivered while the bitter strike raged. *(Y5700)*

The Belfast Dockers' and Carters' Strike Joint Dispute Committee, 1907. The Belfast Strike was accompanied by bitter scenes of riot and intimidation and a cynical campaign of sectarian incitement, but also by enormous solidarity. Eventually Sexton, fearful that the amounts being distributed in strike pay would bankrupt the Union, settled the dispute over Larkin's head. Feeling betrayed, and eager to break free of English leadership, Larkin went on to found the Irish Transport and General Workers' Union in 1909. *(Y8077)*

The unfurling of the Amalgamated Society of Woodworkers banner in the Independent Labour Hall, York Street, on 1 May 1935. The banner is dedicated to 'the late brother' William Walker J.P., member of Belfast 9th Branch, Parliamentary Candidate for North Belfast in 1905 and District Delegate between 1900 and 1911. The unfurling ceremony was carried out by Thomas Barron, Chairman of the ASW Executive Council between 1922 and 1939. In attendance were, from left to right, Loftus Johnston, 7th Branch; Thomas Armstrong, 9th Branch; W. McMeekin, 2nd Branch; Herbert Trotter, Belfast East Branch and M.C.; Harry Midgley, Duncairn Branch; Charles Miller, 5th Branch; and Joseph Kennedy, 8th Branch. *(Y8278)*

6

For Entertainment and Delight

The delightful Miss Minnie Cunningham, one of the Empire Theatre's star turns, poses for a publicity shot in the studios of Charles and Russell, photographers, Belfast. *(47/01/91)*

BBC cabaret girls strutting their stuff at the Grand Central Hotel, Royal Avenue, in 1937. *(Y2648)*

A 'Sale of Slaves' takes place during a performance of the pantomime *Ali Baba and the Forty Thieves* at the Empire Theatre in Victoria Square on 6 December 1936. Note the camel with the number-plate standing to the right of centre stage. *(Y2708)*

The cast of *A Trip to the Isle of Man* pose for a group photograph outside the Belfast studios of the BBC in Linenhall Street on 4 July 1925. The famous writer and theatre impresario Tyrone Guthrie, who joined the BBC in Belfast in 1923, is pictured standing at the right in white shirt sleeves and bow tie. Also in the photograph are Mr and Mrs Richard Hayward; Kitty Murphy; Nellie Wheeler; 'Chattie' Tedlie; and Jimmy Mageean. *(HP10/29/1)*

Staff from Electrolux Ltd, who sold electric cleaners and refrigerators in Riddel's Arcade, enjoying their staff dinner at the Gloucester Café in High Street, July 1936. *(Y2420)*

The Ulster Tourist Development Association having dinner in the Grand Central Hotel, Royal Avenue, in April 1936. *(Y2645)*

Staff of Hoover Ltd, Royal Avenue, in their finery for the Hoover Ball (is it being held by the gentleman seated second left?) at the Carlton Café in Donegall Place, December 1936. *(Y1914)*

Staff of the Monarch Laundry pictured at their office dance, also in the Carlton Café, in April 1930. *(Y1911)*

Window display of E.A. Langrish & Co. Ltd, Cinema and Theatre Furbishers, 31 Donegall Street, March 1931. The first projected moving pictures shown in the north of Ireland stunned patrons of the Empire Theatre on 16 November 1896. The short films were the work of the French cinema pioneers, the Brothers Lumière, and were projected by their British agent, a Frenchman named Trewey. Trewey filmed various scenes in Castle Junction and at the Queen's Bridge on his visit to Belfast, which he showed on his return visit to the city a few weeks later. The pictures had come to town! *(Y2125)*

J. Hogg & Sons' 'Eagle Pharmacy' on York Street, *c.* 1903. Our interest in this image is focused on the adjoining premises of Phillips & Co., Photographic Dealers, who were advertising 'little Nipper' cameras for sale for only 4*s* 6*d*, each under the slogan 'Photography for Everyone'. The growing popularity of photography in Belfast from the end of the nineteenth century meant that by 1909 there were thirty-five businesses offering photographic services and supplies in the city. *(Y2820)*

The interior of Hembry's photographic studio in Donegall Place, 1921. Note the choice of backgrounds offered to his sitters, and the opulent draperies and rugs that were also available. The metal brace standing beside the chair in the centre was placed behind the sitter's head to ensure that they remained motionless during the time it took to make the exposure. *(Y1889)*

This cabinet card photograph of a nun sewing was produced for sale by the Belfast photographic firm of Allison's, which had a studio on Donegall Square. The nun was actually one of the studio's employees, who worked as a retoucher when she wasn't being called upon to model. Cabinet cards such as these were produced for the collectibles market; special, often highly decorative, albums were made by Belfast firms such as Marcus Ward to contain them. Religious topics and personalities were popular subjects, although not all of the cards depicting them were as blatantly contrived as this one. *(47/01/95)*

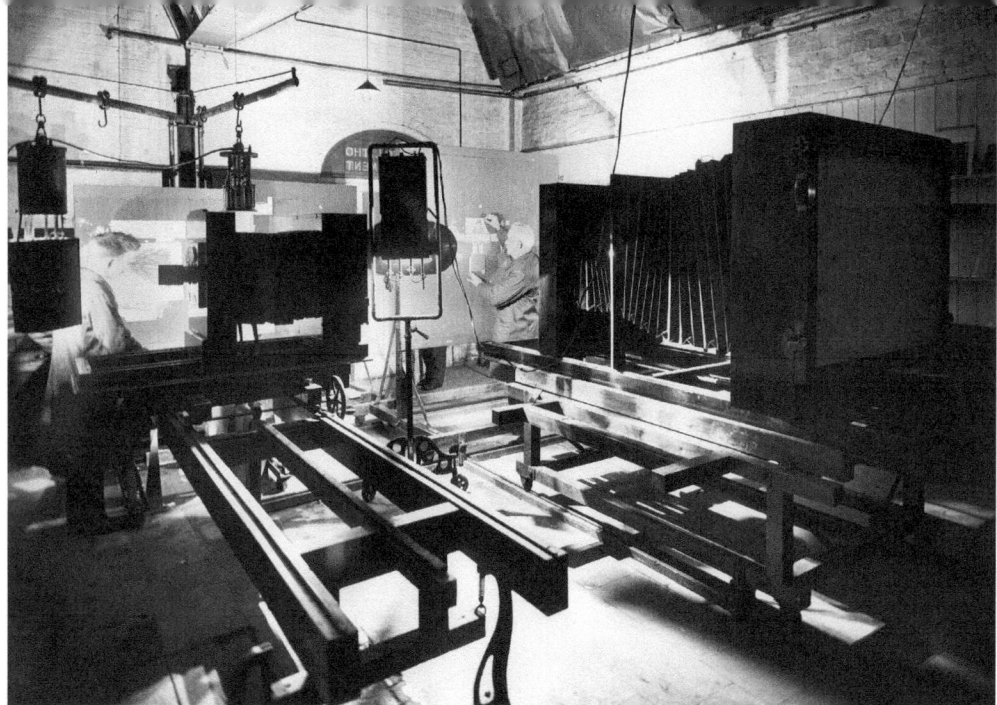

The camera room at McCaw, Stevenson & Orr Ltd, Belfast printers, at their Linenhall Works on the Castlereagh Road, 1925. The development of the half-tone process in the 1890s revolutionised the use of black and white photography in print and publications; by the early 1920s, MSO had perfected its 'Marcotype' process of colour printing, whereby four-colour separations were produced by camera work. Look closely behind the camera to the right of this image to see what appears to be the separated top and bottom halves of one photographer. *(MSO3)*

Another view of McCaw, Stevenson & Orr Ltd in 1925, this time showing the edges of a stone used in lithographic printing being filed and polished. The image on the stone being treated is a 'Glacier' window transparency for third-class railway carriages, one of the many famous lines produced by this highly successful firm. *(MSO11)*

The drawing office at McCaw, Stevenson & Orr Ltd, photographed in 1899, just after the firm had purchased the new works on the Castlereagh Road. The man on the right is drawing elaborate designs for cigarette packaging; the poster above his head advertising Bell's 'Sophia' cigarettes is obviously aimed at the female market for this increasingly popular habit. (W10/58/4)

A group of female workers take a break outside MSO's new building, a huge ex-linen mill known as the Loopbridge Works and quickly rechristened the Linenhall Works, after the printers' previous premises on Linenhall Street. (W10/58/3)

Employees of the famous Belfast firm of Marcus Ward, printers and publishers, photographed in 1868, surrounded by references to the nature and quality of the work they produced. John Ward, one of the founders, is seated in the centre, holding the printed crest of the Prince of Wales; the designer John Vinycombe, pictured as an older man on the facing page, is seated on the extreme right of the second row. *(Y8125)*

For a city its size, Belfast was home to a surprisingly large number of printing concerns besides the two local 'giants' featured earlier. In 1909, for example, the trades directory listed fifty-four firms of printers, including some still-familiar names such as W. & G. Baird, David Allen & Sons, and the Irish News. The firm of Little & McClean, whose letterhead is pictured above, was situated at 65–71 Upper Church Street. *(G9DC5195)*

The talented Marcus Ward designer John Vinycombe, pictured at work in his Holywood studio in 1905. *(H50/04/8)*

The beautiful, leather-bound casket John Vinycombe designed to hold the Marcus Ward-produced illuminated address to Lord Roberts of Kandahar, marking his admission on 9 October 1900 as an honorary Burgess of Belfast in recognition of his successful campaigns in the Transvaal and Orange Free State during the second Boer War. *(H50/04/30)*

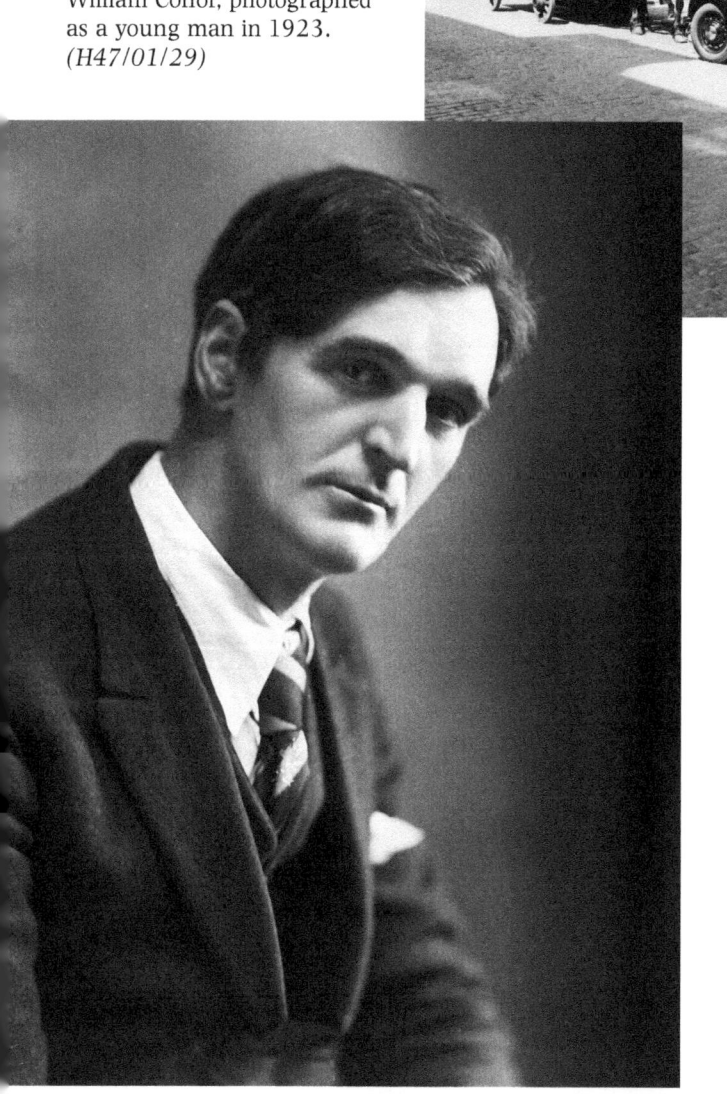

The offices of David Allen & Sons Billposting Ltd in William Street South, photographed in May 1938. The famous and much-loved Belfast artist William Conor served his time here as a graphic designer before travelling to Paris to study painting and drawing. *(Y2809)*

William Conor, photographed as a young man in 1923. *(H47/01/29)*

Opposite: One of Conor's typically affectionate portraits of working-class life in Belfast, infused with the good humour and sensitivity of observation that have endeared his work to so many over the years. *(Women)*

Robert Ponsonby Staples, photographed in 1905 in his studio at 14 Pasadena, Kensington Road, Belfast, at work on one of two triptychs of shipbuilding he painted for the City Hall. The paintings are now in the collections of fine art held at the Ulster Museum. *(H50/01/105)*

Born in Belfast, the famous artist Sir John Lavery began his career in Glasgow and later became one of the most successful portraitists of his generation. He married his second wife, the beautiful Hazel Martyn from Chicago, in 1910 and in 1927 was commissioned to paint an idealised portrait of her as Kathleen Ni Houlihan, which appeared on Irish currency from 1928 until 1975. In 1929 he gave a collection of thirty-six of his paintings, representing the various aspects of his career, to the newly opened Stranmillis Road site of the Belfast Museum and Art Gallery, now the Ulster Museum. This photograph was taken in May of that year and shows Sir John and Lady Hazel standing in the Sir John Lavery gallery in front of its display of his paintings. *(W10/79/67)*

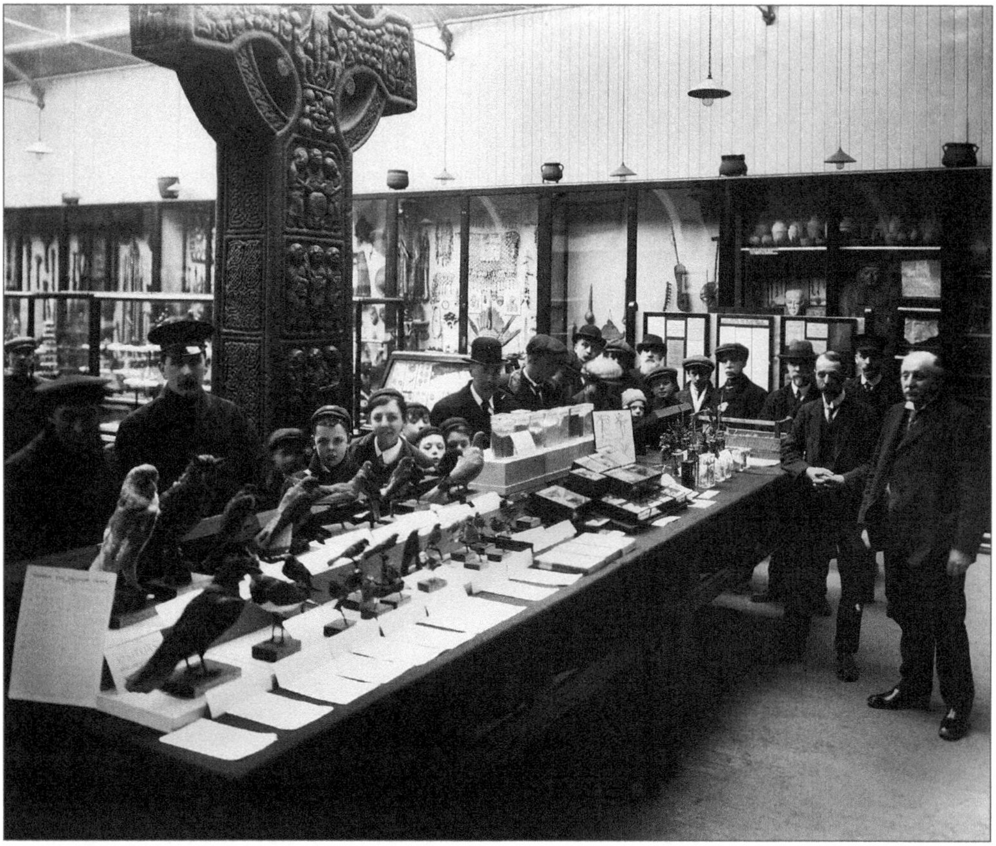

ANCESTRY OF BIRDS
READ THE LABELS IN THE ORDER THEY ARE NUMBERED

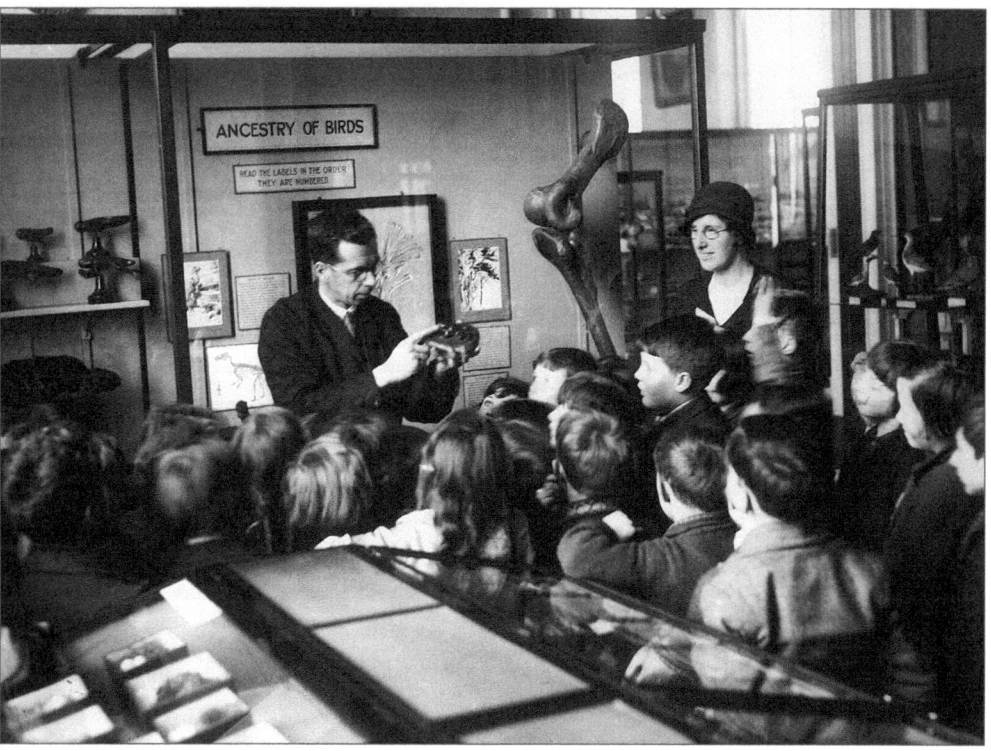

Above: Workmen heave into position the huge bronze temple bell from Thailand that graced the entrance to the Ulster Museum prior to its second refurbishment and reopening in October 2009. *(Y391631)*

Opposite, above: Arthur Deane, pictured on the extreme right, the curator of Belfast Museum and Art Gallery, delivering a lecture on weeds to a group of visitors in 1917, when the Museum was housed in Belfast's Free Public Library on Royal Avenue. In the background can be seen part of the life-size plaster-cast model of the High Cross at Monasterboice, which is still in the Museum's possession. *(Y2666)*

Opposite, below: J.A.S. (Sydney) Stendall, Arthur Deane's Deputy Curator, was appointed Director of the Belfast Museum and Art Gallery in 1942. Here, he is showing what appears to be a cast of a frog to a group of schoolchildren in one of the Museum's natural history galleries. *(Y391630)*

Belfast's Botanic Gardens were established by the Belfast Botanic and Horticultural Society in 1829 on a piece of ground known as the Course, which lay on the north side of the junction of the Stranmillis and Malone roads. They came under the control of Belfast Corporation in 1895, by which time they covered an area of about 17 acres. As well as exhibiting a host of unusual and rare plants, the Gardens secured an increasingly welcome open space for recreation and enjoyment; over the years, they have seen band concerts; fireworks displays; archery demonstrations; balloon ascents; Punch and Judy shows; and even troops of performing Zulus. This photograph was taken in 1902 and shows two men working a horse-drawn lawn mower, under the gaze of a group of children. *(Y7611, detail)*

One of the Gardens' team of groundsmen and gardeners trimming the edge of a bed in front of the magnificent Palm House, designed by the noted architect Charles Lanyon and constructed in stages between 1839, when the foundation stone was laid, and the mid-1850s, when the dome was finally completed. *(Y7610, detail)*

Quick to seize an opportunity, this funfair appeared on a vacant building site at Fisherwick Place in time for the Easter holidays in 1932. The advertising hoardings provide a colourful backdrop for passers-by, while fleets of taxis line the road in front and to the left. Yet the street seems strangely deserted, except for a crowd of children gathered near the Hippodrome on the left. *(Y2219)*

Belfast's streets were full of entertainment, as this delightful image of a balloon man on one of the city's residential streets indicates. Very often, balloons were exchanged for cast-offs, so maybe this is a rag-and-bone man at work. Either way, the prettily dressed little girl he is in conversation with seems entranced by his visit. *(Y7659)*

Acknowledgements

The authors would like to thank the following people for their invaluable help and support in producing this book. We are especially grateful to colleagues and former colleagues at the Ulster Museum: Robert Heslip, Tom Wylie and the late Pauline Dickson of the History Department; Cormac Bourke, Deirdre Crone, Winifred Glover and Sinead McCartan of the Department of Archaeology and Ethnography; Eileen Black, Elizabeth McCrum, Kim Mawhinney and Elise Taylor of the Fine Art and Applied Art Departments; and Peter Crowther and Kenneth James of the Department of Geology for their interest and patience in answering our queries on a range of subjects. Special thanks go to Bryan Routledge and Mike McKeown of the former Photography department in the Ulster Museum for their professionalism, good humour and tolerance as we came to terms with new technologies and processes, and to T. Kenneth Anderson formerly of the Photography department of our sister institution, the Ulster Folk and Transport Museum. Thanks are also due to Patricia McLean, of the Ulster Museum's Marketing department, for her advice on matters relating to copyright. And a special thank you is due to Bill Maguire, erstwhile Keeper of History, Head of the Human History Division and Acting Director of the Ulster Museum whose published and unpublished research on early photography and photographers informed a great part of the text. Ryan Kilpatrick and Sadhbh McGlue's useful research assistance during placements from, respectively, the University of Northumberland and St Dominic's School for Girls, Belfast, was much appreciated. We would also like to thank Sarah Bryce and Alison Miles of Sutton Publishing for their help with the original publication and Tracey Moore of The History Press for her contribution to this reprint.

Responsibility for errors and omissions rests, of course, with the authors, who would be very pleased to receive further information on the images published here. Copies of the images reproduced in this book can be obtained by contacting the Marketing department of the National Museums Northern Ireland.